☐Holdings
Genre _____
Genre _____
☐RFID
☐Final check

SCIENCE NEWS FLASH

WATER

IN THE NEWS

SCIENCE NEWS FLASH

The Environment in the News

Genetics in the News

Medicine in the News

Water in the News

SCIENCE NEWS FLASH

WATER

IN THE NEWS

YAEL CALHOUN

CHELSEA HOUSE
PUBLISHERS

To Aram, who, starting as a young child with the frogs
of Canonchet, has dedicated her life to protecting wetlands.

Water in the News

Copyright © 2007 by Infobase Publishing

Chelsea House
An imprint of Infobase Publishing
132 West 31st Street
New York NY 10001

ISBN-10: 0-7910-9254-2
ISBN-13: 978-0-7910-9254-5

Library of Congress Cataloging-in-Publication Data

Calhoun, Yael.
  Water in the news / Yael Calhoun.
    p. cm. — (Science news flash)
  Includes bibliographical references and index.
  ISBN 0-7910-9254-2 (hardcover)
  1. Water-supply—Juvenile literature. I. Title. II. Series.
  TD348.C25 2007
  333.91—dc22   2006034085

Text design by Annie O'Donnell
Cover design by Ben Peterson

Printed in the United States of America

Bang FOF 10 9 8 7 6 5 4 3 2 1

This book is printed on acid-free paper.

All links and Web addresses were checked and verified to be correct at the time of publication. Because of the dynamic nature of the Web, some addresses and links may have changed since publication and may no longer be valid.

Contents

Oceans

WHAT'S IN THE NEWS?

Fierce hurricanes, global warming, and alternative energy sources are in the news. How do oceans affect global warming or hurricanes? A growing number of scientists believe that hurricanes have become more intense because of global warming (Figure 1.1). Burning fossils fuels, such as coal, oil, and gas, increases the carbon dioxide levels in the atmosphere, which traps more heat and produces the "greenhouse effect." As warmer temperatures heat the oceans, weather patterns and the flow of ocean currents change.[1] Should we shift our energy use from fossil fuels toward alternative sources that do not dump carbon dioxide into the air? Other related news stories concern the pros and cons of storing carbon under the ocean, with the accompanying potential for changing the ocean chemistry.

Pollution is in the news. The U.S. Environmental Protection Agency (EPA) has reported that **nonpoint source pollution** is the number-one source of pollution to our nation's waters.[2] Nonpoint source pollution includes runoff from streets, parking lots, and agricultural areas. Rivers are often fed by lakes or groundwater and then flow into the ocean. Therefore, even freshwater pollution is ocean news. Some scientists estimate that 60 percent of our coastal areas are degraded.[3] Nonpoint source pollution is a major reason why 40 percent of our surveyed rivers, lakes, and estuaries, even 35 years after the passage of the Clean Water Act, still do not meet the standards for fishing or swimming. Science has shown us that air pollution also causes ocean pollution. Airborne mercury from burning fossil fuels falls into our oceans. In 2005, the EPA issued an advisory that cautioned children and pregnant women to limit their intake of certain fish, such as tuna, because of high levels of mercury.[4]

Ocean news also includes the loss of **biodiversity** and the growing number of endangered species. Biodiversity, or the diversity of species on the planet, is a key to keeping our **ecosystems** healthy and to providing resources, such as medicines, for human use. Other ocean-related news items include possible development of cancer drugs from deep-sea creatures and the drowning of dolphins in fishing nets. Possibly millions of species living in the oceans have yet to be identified.[5] Other ocean species are threatened or in danger of becoming extinct.

Overfishing and by-catch (a term used to refer to the animals accidentally caught in fishing nets), contribute to the growing numbers of threatened and endangered species. "The situation in oceans around the world is deteriorating, and at an escalating pace," stated Achim Steiner, director-general of the World Conservation Union (IUCN). "Of the 17 largest fisheries around the world, 15 are at either maximum exploitation levels or are depleting the level of their fish resource base."[6]

For most of time that humans have been pondering such things, people believed the deep oceans were dark, still waters without any life. Recent research has shown that even the deep oceans teem with life. As the ecologist Eugene Odum noted, "This ubiquity of life makes the ocean the largest three-dimensional ecosystem on Earth."[7] Our planet has five major oceans—the Atlantic, the Arctic, the Antarctic, the Pacific, and the Indian—covering about 70 percent of the Earth's surface. More than a billion people rely on the oceans for their primary source of protein. More than half of the world's population lives within 100 miles (161 kilometers) of a coast. Oceans are important not only to the United States but also to the world. That is a lot of news—global news—and understanding the science behind the headlines helps one to understand the issues and how to be part of the solution.

THE SCIENCE

What Are the Ocean Ecosystems?

The oceans are not vast homogeneous bodies of water but are indeed a wondrous, diverse, and dynamic world shaped by a remarkable interplay of physical, chemical, and biological factors. The physical, chemical, and biological differences found within the

Figure 1.1 In August 2005, the Gulf Coast was devastated by Hurricane Katrina, one of the deadliest and most traumatic natural disasters to hit the United States. The photograph above shows extensive flooding of a New Orleans neighborhood two weeks after the hurricane. Although some scientists believe global warming contributed to the fierceness of Hurricane Katrina, it is difficult to prove this theory.

oceans create distinct marine, or ocean, ecosystems. An ecosystem is a community of living things that interact with each other in a particular environment. The "system" includes both the living and nonliving parts. For example, a coral-reef ecosystem includes the plants, animals, microorganisms, soils, water, and weather of the area. Each ecosystem plays a vital role in keeping the planet healthy. Some marine ecosystems include open ocean, coastal areas, coral reefs, deep ocean, mangrove **swamps**, and estuaries.

Ocean waves, currents, temperature, **salinity**, tides, and light are the major physical factors that affect ocean life. The ocean life, from plankton (the microscopic plants and animals) to blue whales, the largest mammals ever to have lived on Earth, in turn, affects both the physical and chemical characteristics of the oceans.

For example, ocean life affects the levels of dissolved gases and builds the ocean **sediment** as organisms decay. Microscopic ocean plants, or phytoplankton, absorb huge amounts of carbon dioxide, which is a **greenhouse gas**, from the atmosphere. Phytoplankton are also a major source of the oxygen that we breathe. Ocean life is, in turn, affected by the physical factors of ocean temperatures, which also play a major role in regulating ocean currents, climate, and local weather patterns.

This physical, chemical, and biological interplay connects each ecosystem to others. The connection among individual ecosystems occurs through complex energy and nutrient cycling. Energy cycling happens through the food webs, as in the case of fish feeding on microscopic plankton and, in turn, being eaten by larger and larger fish or mammals. Nutrients are cycled through complex biological, chemical, and physical routes.[8]

Scientists do not fully understand how the ocean ecosystems work or the full impact of the oceans on the land and the atmosphere. In fact, scientists have gathered more information about the Moon than about our oceans.

Open Ocean

As Rachel Carson observed in 1961, "Unmarked and trackless though it may seem to us, the surface of the ocean is divided into definite zones, and the pattern of the surface water controls the distribution of its life."[9]

Given that the oceans cover approximately 70 percent of the Earth's surface, the open-ocean habitat is a vast expanse. Open oceans are filled with nutrients and populated by creatures that can maneuver across the seemingly endless stretches of water. As in all ecosystems, sunlight is the energy source that powers the system. In the open ocean, sunlight does not penetrate below about .16 miles (250 meters). This depth defines the photic zone, or the area where floating plants can capture energy through **photosynthesis**. The plants form the base of the food chain, meaning that all other life derives energy directly from the plants or from organisms that eat the plants.[10]

Coastal Waters: Continental Shelves, Estuaries, and Coral Reefs

Although most of the oceans are open or deep waters, the coastal ecosystems provide the planet with the richest diversity of species and are the most productive. These edge areas, places in which one ecosystem meets or overlaps with another, are the more dynamic ecosystems. They contain life from the bordering ecosystems and some that is unique to that system. Coastal ecosystems include the continental shelves, estuaries, and coral reefs.

The Earth's crust is made up of plates that move in response to the pressures from deep within the planet. This movement of continental and ocean plates over millions of years has created continental shelves, or shallow ocean areas that ring the continents. Continental shelves are only a small part of the entire ocean floor, yet they generate, by some estimates, trillions of dollars a year in goods and services.[11]

The shape of the ocean basin, ocean temperature, and direction of the prevailing winds directly affect the way the ocean currents move. As winds push surface waters along the edge of the continents, the deeper waters, which are rich in nutrients, move upward. This upwelling of cold, nutrient-rich waters feeds one of the most productive ecosystems on Earth. Because of this food supply, continental shelves serve as nurseries for many fish and invertebrate species. Some scientists estimate that 90 percent of all fish caught come from the third of the ocean that lies within 200 miles (321.8 km) of land—the continental shelves.[12]

At the coastal edge of the continental shelves, freshwater from the land mixes with the saline ocean waters (Figure 1.2). These special places are called estuaries and are formed where rivers empty to the sea, and where tides inundate the coast twice a day with salt water. Chesapeake Bay is our nation's largest **estuary**. It receives half of its water from the Atlantic Ocean and half from water draining from rivers, groundwater, and the land contained

Figure 1.2 Photographed above is the Parker River National Wildlife Refuge, located on the southern portion of a barrier island near Newburyport, Massachusetts. This coastal wetland and estuary serves as a nesting habitat for migratory birds such as Ross's gulls and black swans, in addition to a variety of mammals, reptiles, and amphibians.

in six states and the District of Columbia.[13] Because of the mixing of waters from land and sea, estuaries provide shelter and food for most of the fish that are harvested both near the shore and in other ocean ecosystems.[14]

Salt marshes in the temperate areas and mangrove swamps in the subtropical and tropical areas develop along the land edges, which adds to the diverse life of estuaries. Mangrove trees live in salt water and provide habitat to many fish species, which include many sport and commercial species.[15]

Coral reefs develop in tropical coastal areas and create a unique ecosystem that is home to the highest diversity of ocean species. They are sometimes called the rainforests of the seas. In a given reef, 4,000 species of fish, 800 species of coral, and thousands of other species can be found.[16] The Great Barrier Reef in Australia has more than 200 species of coral alone—one reef may be home to more than 3,000 species of fish, invertebrates, and algae.[17]

Coral reefs are formed as corals, which are animals, secrete calcium carbonate shells that build into the hard reefs. Yet they are not alone—corals live together with tiny plants, or plankton, called zooxanthallae, that capture the energy from the sun as they photosynthesize. In this example of symbiosis, or creatures living together, the corals offer minerals and a sturdy home to the algae, which, in turn, provide food for the corals.

Deep Ocean

The deep ocean is cold and dark, which is why, until the middle of the 1800s, people believed that the waters of the deep ocean did not circulate or contain life. Although light cannot penetrate below about .16 miles (250 m), the deep ocean is filled with life. These deeper layers, below the point where light penetrates, are called the benthic zone. Far from being a dead zone, the ocean floor is rich with life. Creatures adapted to the challenging deep-sea conditions are, by human standards, bizarre. One example is the deep-sea angler fish, which houses bioluminescent bacteria in an appendage used as a fishing lure. By some estimates, between 4 and 11 million species on the planet are as yet unidentified, many of which reside in the oceans.[18]

What powers this ecosystem hidden from sunlight? Gravity provides some energy, as dead plants and animals, with energy stored in their biomass, fall toward the bottom and decompose. Yet, some deep-sea creatures are chemotrophs, which derive energy through chemical processes. An example is sulfur bacteria discovered near a hydrothermal vent in the ocean floor in 1977. Hydrothermal vents form as the ocean crust moves and releases gases, steam, and heat from below. Sulfur bacteria make food from hydrogen sulfide and exist independently of sunlight.[19] Some 400 new species have since been identified near that vent. Such organisms provide the base of a deep-sea food chain.

What Threatens Ocean Ecosystems?

Pollution

Pollution is a major threat to the health of the oceans. The damage can be direct, as in the plant and animal deaths after an oil spill (Figure 1.3). The effects can also be indirect, such as the human health hazard of eating fish laden with mercury from air pollution. Some pollution is visible—plastic and garbage floating in the water—whereas other pollution, such as some toxic compounds, are measured in parts per billion. Pollution threats come from the land, from the sea, and from the air.

Pollution can be from easily identifiable sources, such as a factory discharge pipe, animal feedlots, or an oil spill. In 2002, the EPA estimated that animal feedlots create about 500 million tons (453 million metric tons) of manure every year, which is three times as much sanitary waste as humans in this country produce.[20] Oil spills from tankers have created huge pollution problems. In 1989, the *Exxon Valdez* spilled 10.9 million gallons (41.6 million liters) of crude oil off the coast of Alaska.

Yet, even after the surface oils are removed, toxic compounds remain for many years and are slowly released as the remaining oils in the water and sediment degrade. As an example, oil from a barge spill 30 years ago is still found in the surface sediment in some Massachusetts salt marshes—and even small amounts of these compounds can damage marine organisms.[21]

Other pollution sources include malfunctioning sewage-treatment plants, plant holding tanks that overflow during storm events, and poorly functioning pump stations.[22] One other ocean pollutant is from societies that use materials made from long-chained hydrocarbons—otherwise known as plastics. In some places, the oceans are choked with plastic garbage in forms that strangle mammals or are ingested by, and kill, sea turtles. Even smaller pieces of plastic become pollutants as they absorb toxic

Figure 1.3 In 1989, the Exxon Valdez oil tanker hit the Bligh Reef in Prince William Sound, Alaska. More than 11 million gallons of crude oil emptied into the sea and damaged approximately 745 miles (1,200 km) of Alaskan coastline. In this aerial shot, a skimming barge sucks up some of the oil spillage, and a small fishing boat (*bottom center*) controls a small oil slick.

chemicals and travel the globe, often ingested with plankton by small fish that are then eaten by larger fish that concentrate the toxins in their body tissue. Such bioaccumulation of toxins directly affects human health when people eat fish (such as tuna) or ocean mammals.[23]

The EPA has identified another type of pollution of concern. Nonpoint source pollution is from sources that are not as readily identified, such as runoff from roads and lawns, farmlands, individual septic systems, and boats discharges. Nonpoint source pollution is the chief cause of algal blooms and toxic pollution in the oceans.[24] A 2002 report by the National Research Council found that during the course of one year, the oil washing off our roads and parking lots (totaling 16 million gallons [60.5 million liters] is more than was spilled by the *Exxon Valdez* (10.9 million gallons [41.6 million liters]. Nonpoint source pollution, the report concluded, is the largest pollution source to our coastal areas.[25] Each summer in the Gulf of Mexico, an area the size of Massachusetts becomes anoxic (without oxygen), or a "dead zone," as a result of agricultural runoff.

Supporting this finding about nonpoint source pollution is a 2004 report by the Natural Resources Defense Council (NRDC) that states that local authorities could not identify 68 percent of the pollution sources for their beach closings and advisories.[26] More than 60 percent of our coastal rivers and bays are moderately to severely degraded by nonpoint source runoff.[27]

In addition to oil spills and fertilizers, another type of pollution threatens ocean mammals. A report released by the NRDC in November 2005 stated that increasing levels of noise created by military sonar, shipping, and oil and gas exploration threaten dolphins and whales. Researchers base their findings on examination of beached animals.[28] A federal investigation into the mass stranding of 17 whales in the Bahamas in March 2000 cited the U.S. Navy's use of midfrequency sonar as a contributing factor. "It is a set of symptoms that have never before been seen in marine mammals," said Michael Jasny, the report's principal author. "That physical evidence has led scientists to understand that the sonar is injuring the whales in addition to causing them to strand."[29]

Coastal Development

Nearly half of all the people in the world live within 100 miles (161 km) of a coast (Figure 1.4).[30] More than half of all Americans live in an area, or **watershed**, that drains to the ocean. If the current building pattern in this country continues, by 2015 our coastal population could reach an estimated 165 million people—with another 180 million people visiting each year.[31]

What does this population increase mean for the oceans? Because people live in houses, drive on roads, shop in malls, and work a commutable distance from home, increased population means more pollution. Habitat is destroyed by coastal development. Coastal marshes, which filter pollutants and act as nurseries for many species of wildlife and fish, are increasingly being degraded or destroyed. One estimate states that the United States is losing coastal marshes at about 20,000 acres (81 square km) per

Figure 1.4 This photograph shows Copacabana Beach in southern Rio de Janeiro, Brazil. Approximately 400,000 people live in Copacabana, making it one of the most heavily populated areas in the world.

year. Coastal development had destroyed much of the coastal **wetlands** around New Orleans, wetlands that, in addition to providing a much-needed buffer against Hurricane Katrina, could have filtered much pollution from the land before it entered the coastal areas and ocean.

Habitat Change

Humans, like other animals, use the land and the water to sustain life. Yet humans, owing to their numbers and their personal habits, exact a greater toll than other creatures. As an example, since settling at Plymouth Rock in the 1600s, people have destroyed more than half of all U.S. wetlands, more than 110 million acres (445 sq km).[32]

Habitat loss is considered the number-one cause of species becoming threatened or endangered. Ocean habitats can be lost in many ways. Pollution can make an area unable to sustain life. Because many plants and animals have specific temperature limits in which they can survive, global warming can create habitat loss. Physical destruction, including fishing the ocean bottom with industrial trawls, blasting coral reefs, and offshore drilling, adds to habitat loss.

Loss of Biodiversity

Although species have been going extinct for millions of years, the current rate at which extinction is happening is a major cause for alarm. *Biodiversity* is a term used to describe the biological diversity that exists on three levels: diversity of ecosystems, diversity of species, and diversity of genes. E.O. Wilson, Harvard biologist and Pulitzer Prize winner, explains in his book *The Future of Life* that of the 36 known animal phyla, or classification groups, all 36 phyla occur in the ocean. Only 10 phyla are found on land.[33] Everything that threatens the oceans—pollution, habitat destruction, global warming, overfishing—threatens the diversity of the life in them.

Biodiversity is important for many reasons. A diversity of species keeps an ecosystem healthy, which contributes, in turn, to human health. Healthy ecosystems generate a huge economic return. We are discovering increasing numbers of uses, both medicinal and agricultural, for an increasing number of species. With millions of species as yet undiscovered and increasing amounts of habitat being destroyed, preserving biodiversity has become a key international issue.

Overfishing and By-catch

Historically, humans believed the supply of animals to be endless. However, even as early as the 1920s, people were beginning to see, for example, that the whales were being overhunted. Then, in the 1940s, fishing took on a new face with the introduction of the industrial fishing vessels, or factory ships, complete with radar, acoustic fish finders, synthetic netting, seine nets, and refrigeration capabilities.[34] Now the ocean bottom could be scraped clean by thousands of miles of fishing nets set each day, dragged by ships through the open ocean as deep as one mile (1.6 km). Industrial fishing meant that instead of taking one species of choice, such as tuna or swordfish, all the life within the reach of the nets was captured. It also meant that, according to one study, the amount of fish taken between 1950 and 1992 tripled.[35]

As a direct result of the industrial fishing, the 1960s saw the collapse of major fisheries in Norway and Iceland. In the 1980s, New England fish stocks—cod, haddock, flounder, and halibut—reached historic lows. Globally, 75 percent of the world's major fish stocks are categorized as either overfished or in decline.[36] The Grand Banks off Newfoundland was at one time the most productive fishing area in the world. By the early 1990s, the cod population had dropped to one-hundredth of its former size.[37] The open oceans are feeling the pressure too. During the past 150 years, the large-predator fish population has decreased by 90 percent.[38] Science is showing that industrial fishing is not sustainable fishing (Figure 1.5).

Recently, the U.S. Commission on Ocean Policy concluded after a three-year study that one-fourth of our nation's fish stock, or 257 major species, are overfished. Perhaps a more compelling

Figure 1.5 Greenpeace activists protest the trawler "Ocean Rover" as it operates in the Bering Sea near the Alaska coast. Activists and many concerned scientists believe that factory trawlers are having an adverse effect on the North Pacific ecosystem.

number is the federal government's 2001 report that only a fifth of our fish stocks under federal management were being fished in a manner that could sustain the populations.[39]

Another issue born of industrial fishing is the devastation of by-catch. The term means all the unintentional catch—animals that happened to be in the way of the huge nets. By-catch includes birds, sea turtles, dolphins, otter, and young fish. Richard Ellis, in his book *The Empty Ocean*, notes that the numbers are alarming, with estimates putting the by-catch waste at 25 percent of the catch.[40] The 2004 U.S. Commission on Ocean Policy noted that by-catch is the greatest threat to whales, dolphins, and porpoises.

A 2003 study estimated that more than 300,000 of these mammals are killed around the world each year in fishing gear.

Invasive Species

Invasive species are plants or animals that move into an area in which they do not occur naturally. Once invasive species, such as the zebra mussel or water hyacinth, are established in an ecosystem, the damage has many dimensions. They can damage water systems, destroy recreational opportunities, damage fishing, create public-health problems, and degrade ecosystems. The problem may not be big headline news, but invasive species cause about $137 billion in lost revenue and managements costs in the United States each year.[41]

The methods of introduction can vary—perhaps grass seeds stuck to bags from Europe, mussels or snails clinging to the hull of a ship from Russia, or exotic pets released by individuals in the wild. Another source of invasive species is aquaculture. When fish escape, they can spread disease or outcompete the native fish for food. Aquatic invasive species, such as snails, crabs, jellyfish, and various plants, are of notable concern because ships that carry them are difficult to monitor, and once established, any invasive species is difficult to remove safely.

The EPA reported that invasive species, after habitat destruction, are the primary cause of threatened and endangered species. The rate of introduced species, like the rate of species becoming threatened or going extinct, is of major concern. In the past two centuries, the rate of introduction has increased exponentially.[43] An estimated 7,000 species are transported around the world each day in ballast water (water put in the ship at the beginning of the journey, and then emptied at the point of destination).[44]

Global Climate Change

As John Muir said, "When we try to pick out anything by itself, we find it hitched to everything else in the Universe."[45] A prime example of such connectedness is ocean ecosystems. The energy connection begins with the Sun providing plants, such as plankton, with energy to make food. The Sun also heats the oceans. The important point is that heat trapped within the Earth's atmosphere directly affects ocean currents, which carry the plankton that are the base of the food chain. Ocean currents also affect weather patterns, which have a direct impact on the amount of water and the temperatures in any ecosystem. The Intergovernmental Panel on Climate Control (IPCC), a panel of more than 2,000 international scientists, predicts that over the next century, the Earth could warm by 2.5°F to 10.4°F (1.4°C to 5.8°C).[46] Warmer air means warmer ocean water, which means changes in how ocean currents and the food and heat they carry travel the globe.

Does the direction of ocean currents really matter? Well, compare the climates of Scotland and Labrador, areas that are the same distance north of the equator. Labrador is a frozen land, whereas Scotland has rolling hills of green. The reason is the Gulf Stream, an ocean current that warms the British Isles. As warming waters change the flow of currents, the availability of dissolved substances, such as oxygen and nutrients, could become severely limited in some areas of the ocean. Chemical and physical changes in the ocean could have a direct impact on plankton and, thus, affect the whole ocean food web and decrease productivity along the continental shelves. Warmer waters also dissolve more carbon dioxide, which makes the water more acidic and likely to dissolve the coral reefs.

In addition, further warming will increase the current trend of melting glaciers and ice caps around the world. The IPCC predicts a potential increase in sea level from 4 to 35 inches (9 to 88 centimeters) as glaciers and icecaps melt.[47] Coastal ecosystems will flood, which will alter these key ocean ecosystems. Melting ice will cause an influx of freshwater into the oceans and change both the salinity and water temperature. The changes will directly affect the major ocean currents, such as the Gulf Stream.

A 2004 report on coral reefs, compiled by 240 experts from 98 countries, states that one of the main causes of coral-reef destruction is climate change, which promotes coral bleaching by killing the photosynthetic algae (zooxanthallae) that lives with the coral and provides the coral with food. The report also predicts that the 1998 extreme coral-bleaching event caused by El Niño will become a regular event if global warming trends continue as predicted.[48] Some scientists predict that even a warming of 2°F could destroy the coral reefs of the world.[49]

HISTORY OF THE ISSUE

What Is a Fishing Zone?

People have been sailing the seas for thousands of years. About 400 years ago, countries began claiming fishing rights to the area just off their coasts. Increased fishing pressures and an awareness of the effects of pollution from oil drilling inspired a more formal policy. In 1945, President Harry Truman claimed the continental shelf, an area that extends 12 miles offshore, as the exclusive fishing zone of the United States. In 1983, President Ronald Reagan created the Exclusive Economic Zone (EEZ), which expanded the U.S. jurisdiction to 200 miles (322 km) off the American shores. In response, other countries have followed the American lead. These actions are allowed by the United Nations Convention on the Law of the Sea.[50]

The United Nations Law of the Sea, signed by more than 150 countries, was adopted in 1982. As stated, the law addresses the following:

> Navigational rights, territorial sea limits, economic jurisdiction, legal status of resources on the seabed beyond the limits of national jurisdiction, passage of ships through narrow straits, conservation and management of living marine resources, protection of the marine environment, a marine research regime and, a more unique feature, a binding procedure for settlement of disputes between States.[51]

In 1995, the United Nations Conference on Straddling Fish Stocks and Highly Migratory Fish Stocks came into force. It is an international attempt to regulate fishing in the open oceans.[52]

On the national level, the United States passed the Magnuson-Stevens Fishery Conservation and Management Act in 1976, in an effort to regulate fishing. The law set up regional fishery management councils to ensure participation by industry, states, and public groups. The law also requires that the act be periodically updated. It was reauthorized in 1996 (Public Law 94-265) and is before the 2007 Congress for reauthorization.

The United States was not alone in addressing the problems of decreased fishing stocks. The 1970s saw fishing regulations developed in Europe to establish fishing grounds and to designate markets. In 1983, the European Union established the Common Fisheries Policy (CFP) to deal with conserving fish stocks and set-ting market policy.[53] In 2002, the European Union designated the entire Mediterranean Sea as off-limits to large-scale drift nets.[54]

What Protects Whales? (International Whaling Commission)

Recognizing that the whales were being overhunted, concerned nations established the International Whaling Commission (IWC) in 1946. The stated purpose of the IWC was "to provide for the orderly development of the whaling industry." In 1986, the IWC expanded its reach and called for a complete halt to whaling until the stocks could be declared safe for harvest. The moratorium on whale hunting is still in effect, yet Norway, Iceland, and Japan refuse to comply. These nations use loopholes in the regulations to continue hunting.

The IWC Scientific Committee draws from 200 of the world's leading whale biologists. Recently, the committee's study has expanded to include environmental issues. Today, 66 nations have signed the agreement.[55]

What Protects Endangered Species in the Oceans? (CITES)

CITES (referred to as *SITE-eez*; the Convention on International Trade in Endangered Species of Wild Fauna and Flora) was the result of international concerns in the 1960s about protecting threatened and endangered plants and animals. CITES came into force in 1975, and today 169 countries have voluntarily signed the legally binding agreement that protects more than

30,000 species of plants and animals from illegal harvest and trade. Among the many ocean species protected by CITES are the entire group of cetaceans (whales, dolphins, and porpoises) and sea turtles.[56]

The World Conservation Union (IUCN) has developed the IUCN Red List of Threatened Species that provides taxonomic (classification) and conservation information on threatened or endangered plants and animals of the world.[57] CITES uses the Red List to identify species that need protection.

How Does the Clean Water Act Protect Oceans?

The first action by the federal government to control water pollution was the Federal Water Pollution Control Act of 1972. After being amended in 1977, it became known as the Clean Water Act (CWA). The act was a significant step toward cleaning the nation's polluted waters. The CWA regulates pollutant discharges, establishes industry standards for wastewater, and sets water-quality standards for surface water. Section 402 regulates point-source pollution discharges into any "navigable waters," such as discharge pipes from industry or sewage-treatment plants. Permits that require the use of state-of-the-art technology must be obtained before any discharges are allowed.

Section 404 of the CWA regulates the use of wetlands, including the coastal marshes and estuaries. Protecting coastal wetlands, which act as biological filters of pollutants, also serves to protect ocean ecosystems and water quality.[58]

What Other Regulations Protect Ocean Resources?

Coastal Zone Management Act of 1972 (CZMA)

In 1972, the federal government established a program to give technical assistance and funding to coastal states and territories to develop coastal management plans in an effort to manage coastal development. The CZMA states that development within coastal areas must be consistent with the state's coastal zone management plan.

The Marine Mammal Protection Act of 1972

The Marine Mammal Protection Act (MMPA) of 1972 was established in response to the public outcry over the clubbing of seals, the killing of whales, and the strangling of dolphins in tuna nets. The MMPA provides protection for marine mammals in the waters of the United States and prohibits American citizens from killing them in any ocean. The act is periodically amended, and the last amendment was in 1997.

The Ocean Dumping Act of 1972

The Marine Protection, Research, and Sanctuaries Act of 1972 gives the federal government power to regulate ocean dumping and disposal of all materials in U.S. waters. The law had to be amended in 1988 to specifically halt the disposal of sewage sludge and industrial wastes into American oceans.

National Invasive Species Act (NISA)

No policy was in place to address the problem of invasive aquatic species until 1990, when Congress passed the Nonindigenous Aquatic Nuisance Prevention and Control Act of 1990 (NANPCA). It attempted to prevent the introduction of invasive species and to control the spread of others. In 1996, the law was strengthened and the name changed to the National Invasive Species Act of 1996.

Marine Protected Areas

In 1972, the United States launched the only protection program designed specifically to protect marine resources by establishing the U.S. Marine Sanctuary Program (Figure 1.6), a program similar to our National Park and Wilderness Area designations on land. The intention was to set aside sections of the ocean ecosystems that would be protected from oil drilling and mining, while allowing some recreational activities. The official definition of a marine protected area (MPA) refers to "any area of the marine environment that has been reserved by federal, state, territorial, tribal, or local laws or regulations to provide lasting protection for part or all of the natural and cultural resources within them."[59]

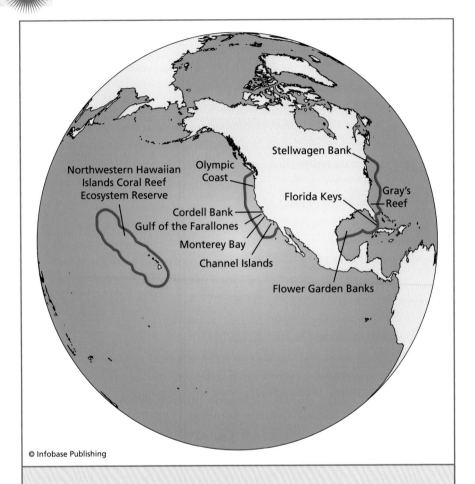

Northwestern Hawaiian Islands Coral Reef Ecosystem Reserve

Olympic Coast

Stellwagen Bank

Gray's Reef

Florida Keys

Cordell Bank
Gulf of the Farallones

Monterey Bay

Channel Islands

Flower Garden Banks

© Infobase Publishing

Figure 1.6 Marine Protected Areas were first designated in 1972. The goal was to protect vital marine ecosystems. A sampling of MPAs are indicated in the map above.

An even greater degree of protection, with no fishing or extraction activities allowed, is given to much smaller areas designated as marine reserves. An example of such an area covers 6 percent of the 2,900 square nautical miles (9,950 sq km) of the Florida Keys National Marine Sanctuary, established in 1990. Results have shown that creation of these protected areas improves the ecosystem health, and with that improvement comes many economic and related environmental benefits.[60]

The United States is not alone in protecting marine areas. In 1981, the Great Barrier Reef in Australia—an area larger than the United Kingdom, the Netherlands, and Switzerland combined—was declared a World Heritage Area, which makes Australia home to the largest marine protected area in the world (Figure 1.7).[61] New Zealand, Belize, the Dominican Republic, the Philippines, and some countries in Africa and Europe have also established marine protected areas.

CURRENT ISSUES AND FUTURE CONSIDERATIONS

Over the years, the United States has enacted more than 140 different laws and regulations. Six different federal agencies, with more than 20 departments, oversee ocean issues. The result is a lack of coordination in ocean policy and implementation of regulations. The current challenge, as outlined by the U.S. Presidential Commission, is to establish a "unifying vision of ocean stewardship."[62]

The common call for a unifying vision is echoed by such international organizations as the World Summit on Sustainable Development, the World Parks Congress, and the Convention on Biological Diversity. The global challenge is to develop a network of marine protected areas, to implement sustainable fishing practices, and to establish ecosystem-based management plans to protect the ocean fisheries and ecosystems. The organizations agree that we are running out of time to implement the protection strategies.

What Are the Current Reports on the State of the Oceans?

Two major reports have been issued recently, the first effort in more than 35 years to review the status of the world's oceans: the

Figure 1.7 The Great Barrier Reef, located off the coast of Queensland in north-east Australia, is the world's largest coral reef system. The country of Australia is responsible for protecting and conserving the Great Barrier Reef due to its natural importance in the world.

2003 Pew Oceans Commission's *America's Living Oceans: Charting a Course for Sea Change* [63] and the 2004 U.S. Commission on Ocean Policy's *An Ocean Blueprint for the 21st Century.*[64] Both reports highlight a clear change from any past attempts to grapple with ocean issues—attempts that were largely piecemeal and dealt with issues individually as they became serious. Both reports take a comprehensive look at our ocean resources and outline clear plans for sustainable use. Sustainability, or the use of resources without depleting them, is becoming a key to responsible planning in order to maintain healthy and productive ecosystems. Sustainability demands a shift in thinking from believing we can take whatever we want from the oceans toward practicing responsible stewardship of both the land and the waters.

America's Living Oceans: Charting a Course for Sea Change drew from the expertise of leading scientists, philanthropists, and people in the fishing industry and business. The central issues addressed are policy, fishing, pollution, and coastal development. The report carefully develops an ecosystem approach and considers all that is necessary to assure a sustainable and healthy ecosystem. The report recommends a comprehensive set of strategies to tackle the serious problems.

An Ocean Blueprint for the 21st Century is a comprehensive look at the way we manage our coasts, the Great Lakes, and the oceans, with the intention of providing "a blueprint for change in the twenty-first century, with recommendations for creation of an effective national ocean policy that ensures sustainable use and protection of our oceans, coast, and Great Lakes for today and far into the future." It contains 212 specific recommendations that encompass every aspect of ocean and coastal policy.

In response to *An Ocean Blueprint for the 21st Century*, President Bush established a Committee on Ocean Policy in December of 2004. At the time, the commission chair, U.S. Navy Admiral James D. Watkins, made the following statement:

> I am confident that ocean and coastal issues will be identified as a national priority when the 109th Congress convenes. With a clear mandate from the President, and strong, bipartisan support

among Members of Congress, we can begin the difficult, but critical process of implementing a comprehensive national ocean policy.[65]

The commission recommends that we develop an ecosystem-based management approach by focusing on the following:

A new, coordinated national ocean policy framework to improve decision making.

Cutting-edge ocean data and science translated into high-quality information for managers.

Lifelong ocean-related education to create well-informed citizens with a strong stewardship ethic.[66]

As a result of these key reports, a 10-member task force, with 5 representatives from each commission (the Pew Oceans Commission and the U.S. Commission on Ocean Policy) was established in 2004–2005. The primary goal of the Joint Ocean Commission Initiative is to accelerate ocean-policy reform that targets the core priorities outlined in the two reports.[67] These commissions bring an unprecedented array of expertise to dealing with the critical issues of today's oceans. As stated by the Honorable Leon E. Panetta, commission cochair:

The failure to act expeditiously on these recommendations threatens the economic and ecological health of our oceans, coasts and Great Lakes, whose resources and services are fundamental contributors to the U.S. economy, national security, and quality of life.[68]

A similar urgency is noted in the warnings of Admiral Watkins:

More action is needed now—to implement a national strategy to protect, maintain and restore the nation's priceless economic and ecological assets—our oceans, coasts and Great Lakes . . . We must accelerate the implementation of and increase the funding for policies and science that will help protect and enhance the value of the oceans for the long haul, before it is too late.[69]

In 2006, the chairs of both commissions released reports stating that the government is seriously failing to support their recommendations. The challenge will be to gain the congressional funding needed to realize the goals.

Economics

During the past century, our government encouraged resource development, due to the belief that the only result would be a stronger economy. On the land, people were encouraged to drain and fill wetlands to create more farmland and to log forests to feed our nation's growing need for lumber. 50 years ago, the government supported a similar development of ocean resources, due to the belief that the seas were endless supplies of riches. Just as science showed that pesticides and pollution were killing the land and making us sick, science has also shown that the oceans have limits: limits on what we can take and limits to how much we can pollute.

Science has shown that unrestrained resource consumption and extraction leads to degraded or even failed ecosystems. The results have direct economic consequences in the form of collapsed fisheries, loss of tourism, loss of biodiversity, and degraded ecosystems.

What is the economic value of the oceans? According to the 2004 government report, estimates from the year 2000 state that ocean-related activities generated more than $117 billion for our economy and created more than 2 million jobs. If the coastal areas are included, the economic value increases to more than $1 trillion annually. Commercial fishing alone exceeds $28 billion, and saltwater recreational fishing generates about $20 billion. Recreational boating pumped $30 billion into the 2002 U.S. economy.[70] Healthy coral reefs feed a huge tourist industry, worth billions of dollars a year, in the Florida Keys alone.[71] In addition, coral-reef resources and activities in the United States and its territories add an estimated $375 billion to the U.S. economy every year.[72]

Regulation, and, therefore, revitalization, of the American fishing industry has been estimated to add at least $1.3 billion dollars to the United States' economy. The seafood industry supports 250,000 jobs, and sport fishing creates 350,000 jobs.[73] Oceans are not an economic issue only in the United States. In 69 developing countries, tourism revenues provided one of the five largest inputs of foreign currency between 1995 and 1998.[74]

Whale watching (of live whales in their natural habitat) is a high-profile example of sustainable economic returns from the oceans (Figure 1.8). Whale-watching tourism was estimated to have earned at least $1 billion (U.S. dollars) in income in 2000, double its value from 1996. Whale-watching operations now occur in at least 87 countries and attract more than 9 million people. Is it

Figure 1.8 Whale watchers take notice of an orca surfacing in the Straits of Juan de Fuca. Juan de Fuca Strait and Hairo Strait are the two most popular whale-watching sites in British Columbia, Canada. In addition to orcas, gray whales and humpbacks can be seen trolling the waters.

growing? The number of people watching whales has increased 12 percent each year since 1991.[75,76]

Does protection of ocean resources pay? As an example, consider the tourist-driven economy of Bonair off the coast of Venezuela. A marine park was established in the early 1980s to protect their tourist industry, which is primarily diving. In 1991, the marine park cost about $600,000 to operate. For that year alone, the revenues were $23.2 million. Such economic returns are not unusual in marine protected areas.[77]

Another face to the economic issues is the amount of money spent on scientific research. Strong science has been the basis for formulation of environmental regulations: global warming, clean air, and clean water are examples. The Pew report notes that for more than a decade, federal dollars allocated to oceanic-research issues were about $755 million a year. The committee recommends that the funding for basic research to ensure a sustainable resource be increased to $1.5 billion a year, which is 7 percent of the federal research budget.[78] Both the Pew report and the U.S. Commission on Ocean Policy's report recommend an increase in federal spending for ocean research.

Are Fishing Regulations Important?

Resources that are not owned by a particular person but are owned by many are referred to as "commons." Without international cooperation and oversight, resources, such as the open ocean, can be overused and exploited and eventually ruined, which would lead to what the biologist Garrett Hardin termed "the tragedy of the commons."[79] Examples of this tragedy are depleted whale populations and predator-fish populations that have been decreased by 90 percent from overfishing.

Even today, there is not much known about the status of most of the fish populations that are being heavily fished. Only one-third of the species caught in U.S. waters has been assessed. Of the assessed species, about half were either overfished or about to be overfished.[80] Even less is known about the fish populations in the open oceans.

New regulations and policies reflect our understanding of limited resources: the 1996 Sustainable Fisheries Act brought the new language of "sustainable yield" into our fishing laws. It is part of the U.S. law to set catch limits that allow a particular fish species to maintain itself.[81]

In November of 2005, The United Nations reaffirmed the Convention of the Law of the Sea relating to the conservation and management of straddling fish stocks and migratory fish stocks:

> [T]he importance it attaches to the long-term conservation, management and sustainable use of the marine living resources of the world's oceans and seas and the obligations of States to cooperate to this end, in accordance with international law, as reflected in the relevant provisions of the Convention . . . .[82]

In addition, the European Union has been reviewing and strengthening their fisheries policies since 2003.

The challenge is to implement the recommendations of the Pew Oceans Commission and the U.S. Commission on Ocean Policy in this country and the new fisheries policy of the European Union adopted in 2003. Whether the problems of overfishing will be successfully addressed through legislation, improved fishing practices, and consumer awareness remains to be seen. Whether such measures will be applied in time to save ocean life, most of which has yet to even be identified, also remains to be seen.

What Management Strategies Protect Ocean Resources?

Protected Areas

Marine protected areas (MPAs) are seen by many as a valuable tool for protecting ocean resources and reestablishing the world fisheries. During the past 20 years, science has shown that MPAs have multiple benefits: protecting biodiversity (the number of species), increasing both the fisheries and tourism, and decreasing by-catch. A reflection of this understanding is that the majority of the marine parks today, which number in the hundreds, were set up in the past 20 years.

As the scientific evidence of fisheries in trouble mounts, people are looking more closely at the benefits of closing certain areas to fishing to allow fish populations to recover. A study of the fishery effects of marine reserves and fishery closures in 16 marine reserves confirmed many of the predicted benefits of reserves—increases in spawning stock, increased catches, and increased reproduction among them:

> We demonstrate that the case that reserves benefit fisheries has become much stronger over the last two to three years and fishers and reserve managers can approach reserve implementation with newfound confidence. People contemplating reserve creation can take heart from the experiences of others who are further along in the process. Their experiences prove that reserves can work successfully across a wide range of ecological and socio-economic conditions.[83]

The future concern is that today less than 1 percent of the ocean is protected from certain types of uses. Only about one ten-thousandth of the sea is protected from all fishing, according to Dr. Fiona Gell of the University of York.[84] In a global effort to increase that number, the World Summit on Sustainable Development, the World Parks Congress, and the Convention on Biological Diversity all support the goal of designating a global network of marine protected areas by 2012, including on the open-ocean ecosystems.[85]

Business, Government, and Partnership Initiatives

Oceans have no national boundaries, so the problems of the oceans are shared by the world. Solving large problems has proved more effective when agencies, businesses, and organizations pool resources and work together. The strategy has forged many successful and diverse partnerships.

The Ocean Conservancy recently teamed up with the Coca-Cola Company to sponsor an international beach cleanup. The

World Wildlife Fund, an international conservation organization, works with industries and regional fisheries worldwide to help reduce by-catch. An example of the success of one program, changing from J-hooks to circle hooks, reduced marine turtle by-catch by 90 percent without decreasing the fisheries' catch.

The U.S. Environmental Protection Agency recently awarded a $500,000 grant to the Partnership for the Delaware Estuary for education, outreach, and water-quality improvements. "This partnership effort exemplifies how government and private organizations can come together to support vibrant programs to protect and enhance the critical Delaware Estuary that provides habitat to numerous wildlife species," said Donald S. Welsh, regional administrator for EPA's mid-Atlantic region.[86]

Sometimes large companies make decisions that reflect a commitment to ocean conservation. In the summer of 2005, the Disney Corporation dropped shark-fin soup from their menu. Today, many shark species are threatened because of the fishing practice of cutting off shark fins and throwing the fish back into the ocean.

Just as state governments are forming alliances to fight air pollution, New England's governors, with the support of the NOAA (National Oceanic and Atmospheric Administration), have formed a regional council to coordinate ocean policies. The group will coordinate with a similar Canadian council.

WHAT THE INDIVIDUAL CAN DO

The oceans are huge, and solving the many problems facing them can seem overwhelming. Each of us can do our part to help protect the oceans. Small changes in our everyday habits can help keep our oceans, and our planet, healthy. Helping to solve one problem also helps solve another because, just as John Muir noted, everything is hitched to everything else:

* Reduce, reuse, and recycle. Buy products with less packaging and recycle containers. This practice cuts

down on solid waste (and plastics ending up in the oceans) and reduces energy costs. Reduced energy means less carbon dioxide in the air and less global warming.

* Grow lawns that use less fertilizers, pesticides, herbicides, and water. The result is less runoff into the rivers, lakes, and oceans.

* Use less electricity. Turn lights off and turn the heat and air conditioning down. Many power plants burn fossil fuels, which add carbon dioxide to the atmosphere.

* Drive less. Ride a bike, car pool, or use mass transit instead. Cars pollute the atmosphere and contribute to global warming.

* Support "ecotourism." When you travel, stay at places that respect the environment.

* Let your money talk. Before buying products, find out where they come from. Buy fish that are fished in a sustainable way. Do not buy products from fragile ecosystems such as coral reefs.

* Help out in your community. Even if you live inland, you are connected to the oceans. Volunteer for river or stream monitoring, river cleanups, or recycling efforts. If your community does not have any of these activities, start one yourself.

REFERENCES

1. "Carbon captures & sequestration technologies," MIT. Available online. URL: http://sequestration.mit.edu/technology_overview/index.html. 2005.

2. U.S. EPA. "Nonpoint source pollution: The nation's largest water quality problem," EPA841-F-96-004A. Available online. URL: http://www.epa.gov/owow/nps/facts/point1.htm. 2004.

3. Natural Resources Defense Council. "Testing the waters 2004: A guide to water quality at vacation beaches," Available online. URL: http://www.nrdc.org/water/oceans/ttw/titinx.asp.

4. U.S. EPA. "Fish advisory: What you need to know about mercury and shellfish." Available online, URL: http://www.epa.gov/waterscience/fishadvice/advice.html. 2005.

5. Wilson, E.O. *The Future of Life*. New York: Vintage Books. 2003.

6. Byrnes, Michael. "Scientists draft blueprint to protect world oceans," Reuters News. Available online. URL: http://today.reuters.com/News/CrisesArticle.aspx?storyId=SYD338241). October 25, 2005.

7. Odum, Eugene and Gary W. Barrett. *Fundamentals of Ecology*. Belmont, Calif.: Brooks Cole/Thomson: 2004.

8. Pauly, Daniel and Jay Maclean. *In a Perfect Ocean: The State of Fisheries and Ecosystems in the North Atlantic Ocean*. Washington, D.C.: Island Press, 2003.

9. Carson, Rachel. *The Sea Around Us*. New York: Oxford University Press, 1952.

10. Odum, *Fundamentals of Ecology*.

11. Fujita, Rod. *Heal the Ocean: Solutions for Saving Our Seas*. Gabriola, BC, Canada: New Society Publishers, 2003.

12. Ibid., p. 127.

13. "Chesapeake Bay program." Available online. URL: http://www.chesapeakebay.net/about.htm. 2004.

14. Johnson, George. *The Living World*. 3rd Edition. Boston: McGraw Hill. 2003.

15. Mitch, William J. and James G. Gosselink. *Wetlands*. 3rd Edition. New York: John Wiley & Son, 2000.

16. "Healthy coral reefs," NOAA. Available online. URL: http://coralreef.noaa.gov/outreach/protect/supp_habitat.html.asdf. 2004.

17. Audesirk, Teresa, and Gerald Audesirk. *Biology: Life On Earth.* Upper Saddle River, NJ: Prentice Hall, 1996.

18. Wilson, *The Future of Life*, p. 14.

19. Odum, *Fundamentals of Ecology*, p. 420.

20. *An Ocean Blueprint for the 21st Century.* Washington, D.C.: U.S. Commission on Ocean Policy, 2004.

21. Rabalais, Nancy. "Oil in the sea," *Issues in Science and Technology* Fall 2003.

22. Dorfman, Mark. *Testing the Waters 2004: A Guide to Water Quality at Vacation Beaches.* New York: Natural Resources Defense Council, 2005.

23. Moore, Charles. "Trashed: Across the Pacific Oceans, plastics, plastics, everywhere." *Natural History* 112, no. 9, November 2003.

24. *An Ocean Blueprint for the 21st Century.* Washington, D.C.: U.S. Commission on Ocean Policy, 2004.

25. Pew Oceans Commission. "America's living oceans: Charting a course for sea change." Available online. URL: http://www.pewoceans.org. 2003.

26. Dorfman, Mark. *Testing the Waters 2004: A Guide to Water Quality at Vacation Beaches,* New York: Natural Resources Defense Council, 2005.

27. Pew Oceans Commission. "America's living oceans: Charting a course for sea change." Available online. URL: http://www.pewoceans.org. 2003.

28. Chavez, Paul. "Oceans getting too noisy for dolphins and whales," The Associated Press. Available online. URL: http://seattlepi.nwsource.com/national/249282_oceannoise22.htmlOceans. November 22, 2005.

29. Ibid.

30. The Nature Conservancy. "World ocean day. World ocean facts 2005." Available online. URL: http://nature.org/initiatives/marine/about/art15524.html.

31. Pew Oceans Commission. "America's living oceans: Charting a course for sea change." Available online. URL: http://www.pewoceans.org. 2003.

32. *An Ocean Blueprint for the 21st Century.* Washington, D.C.: U.S. Commission on Ocean Policy, 2004.

33. Wilson, *The Future of Life*, p. 15.

34. Pauley and Maclean, *In a Perfect Ocean*, p. 12.

35. "Wave of marine species extinctions feared," *Washington Post.* Available online. URL: www.washingtonpost.com. 8/24/05.

36. World Wildlife Fund. "Working to reduce fisheries by-catch." Available online. URL: http://worldwildlife.org/oceans/projects/bycatch.pdf. 2005.

37. Wright, Richard T. *Environmental Science: Toward a Sustainable Future.* Upper Saddle River, NJ: Pearson/Prentice Hall. 2005.

38. The World Conservation Union. "Conserving biodiversity. Factsheet." Available online. URL: http://www.iucn.org/themes/wcpa/theme/conserving.html. 2004.

39. Pew Oceans Commission "America's living oceans: Charting a course for sea change." Available online. URL: http://www.pewoceans.org. 2003.

40. Ellis, Richard. *The Empty Ocean: Plundering the World's Marine Life.* Washington, D.C.: Island Press.

41. Pew Oceans Commission. "Invasive species." Available online. URL: http://www.pewtrusts.org/pdf/env_oceans_species.pdf. 2003.

42. Cangelosi, Allegra. "Blocking invasive aquatic species," *Issues in Science and Technology* Winter 2002-2003.

43. Ibid.

44. Pew Oceans Commission. "Invasive species." Available online. URL: http://www.pewtrusts.org/pdf/env_oceans_species.pdf. 2003.

45. Muir, John. *My First Summer in the Sierra.* Boston: Houghton Mifflin, 1911 (Sierra Club Books 1988 edition).

46. Intergovernmental Panel on Climate Change. "Third annual report: Climate change 2001: A Scientific Basis," IPCC. Available online. URL: http://www.grida.no/climate/ipcc_tar/wg1/028.htm#e8. 2001.

47. Intergovernmental Panel on Climate Change. "Third assessment report: Climate change 2001: Synthesis Report: Summary for Poli-

cymakers," IPCC. Available online. URL: http://www.ipcc.ch/pub/
un/syreng/spm.pdf. 2001.

48. Wilkinson, Clive. *Status of Coral Reefs of the World*, Vol. 1. Darwin, Australia: Australian Institute of Marine Science, 2004.

49. Pew Oceans Commission. "America's living oceans: Charting a course for sea change." Available online. URL: http://www.pewtrusts.org/pdf/env_oceans_species.pdf. 2003.

50. United Nations Division for Ocean Affairs and The Law of the Sea. "The United Nations convention on the law of the sea." Available online. URL: http://www.un.org/Depts/los/convention_agreements/convention_historical_perspective.htm#Exclusive%20Economic%20Zone. Updated March 16, 2006.

51. "Oceans and law of the sea: the UN convention of the law of the sea." Available online. URL: http://www.un.org/Depts/los/convention_agreements/convention_historical_perspective.htm#Historical%20Perspective. 2004

52. "Oceans and law of the sea: United Nations conference on straddling fish stock and highly migratory fish stock." Available online. URL: http://www.un.org/Depts/los/fish_stocks_conference/fish_stocks_conference.htm2003.

53. "Fisheries and maritime affairs. Fact sheet: 2.2 The common fisheries policy." Available at: http://europa.eu.int/comm/fisheries/doc_et_publ/factsheets/facts/en/pcp2_2.htm. 2003.

54. World Wildlife Fund. "Marine success stories." Available online. URL: http://www.panda.org/about_wwf/what_we_do/marine/successes/news.cfm?uNewsID=19545. February, 2005.

55. IWC Information. Available online. URL: http://www.iwcoffice.org/commission/iwcmain.htm#nations. 2005.

56. "The CITES species." Available online. URL: http://www.cites.org/eng/disc/species.shtml Marine Protected Areas. 2005.

57. "2004 IUCN red list of endangered species." Available online. URL: http://www.redlist.org. 2005.

58. EPA Law and Regulations. "Clean Water Act." EPA. Available online. URL: http://www.epa.gov/region5/water/cwa.htm. 2005.

59. "MPA executive order 13158." Available online. URL: http://www.mpa.gov/inventory/about_inventory.html). 2000.

60. Klingener, Nancy. "Providing sanctuary," *Blue Planet* Fall 2002.

61. Great Barrier Reef Marine Park Authority (GBRMPA). Available online. URL: http://www.gbrmpa.gov.au/index.html.

62. Natural Resources Defense Council. "Ocean rescue." Available online. URL: http://www.nrdc.org/media.pressrelease/040721. asp. 2004.

63. Pew Oceans Commission. "America's living oceans: Charting a course for sea change." Available online. URL: http://www. pewtrusts.org/pdf/env_oceans_species.pdf. 2003.

64. *An Ocean Blueprint for the 21st Century*. Washington, D.C.: U.S. Commission on Ocean Policy, 2004.

65. U.S. Commission on Ocean Policy. Press Release. Available online. URL: http://www.oceancommission.gov/newsnotices/dec17_04. html. 2004.

66. *An Ocean Blueprint for the 21st Century*. Washington, D.C.: U.S. Commission on Ocean Policy, 2004.

67. "Joint Ocean Commission initiative." Available online. URL: http://www.jointoceancommission.org. 2005.

68. Press Release. U.S. Newswire. Available online. URL: http://releases. usnewswire.com/GetRelease.asp?id=58391. December 19, 2005.

69. Ibid.

70. *An Ocean Blueprint for the 21st Century*. Washington, D.C.: U.S. Commission on Ocean Policy, 2004.

71. "Coral reef conservation program fact sheets." NOAA. Available online. URL: www.coralreef.noaa.gov/. 2006.

72. "Marine sanctuaries fact sheets." NOAA. Available online. URL: www.sanctuaries.nos.noaa.gov/. 2006.

73. Environmental Defense. "Oceans alive." Available online. URL: http://actionnetwork.org.campaign/voerfish2/explanation. 2005.

74. Troëng, S. and Drews C. "Money talks: Economic aspects of marine turtle use and conservation." Available online. URL: http://assets.panda.org/downloads/moneytalks.pdf. 2004.

75. Hoyt, Erich. "Whale watching 2001," International Fund for Animal Welfare. Available online. URL: http://www.ifaw.org/ifaw/general/default.aspx?oid=10196. 2004.

76. Department of Conservation. "Te papa atawhai. The conservation of whales." Available online. URL: http://www.doc.govt.nz/Conservation/001~Plants-and-Animals/003~Marine-Mammals/

Whales/100~Conservation-of-whales-in-the-21st-century/
220~Whale-watching.asp. 2004.

77. Woods Hole Oceanographic Institution. "Marine protected areas,"
    Ocean Life Institute. Available online. URL: http://www.whoi.edu/
    institutes/oli/currenttopics/ct_mpa_econ_ben_mpa.htm. 2006.

78. Pew Oceans Commission. "America's living oceans: Charting
    a course for sea change." Available online. URL: http://www.
    pewtrusts.org/pdf/env_oceans_species.pdf. 2003.

79. Hardin, Garrett. "The Tragedy of the Commons," *Science* 62
    (1968): 1243–1248.

80. Report to Congress. "Status of fisheries of the United States."
    National Marine Fisheries Service. Available online. URL:
    www.nmfs.noaa.gov/sfa/Status%20of%20Fisheries%202000.
    pdf. 2001.

81. Safina, Carl. "The continued dangers of overfishing." *Issues in
    Science and Technology.* Summer 2003.

82. United Nations General Assembly. "Sixtieth session. Agenda
    item 75." Available online. URL: http://daccessdds.un.org/doc/
    UNDOC/GEN/N05/612/18/PDF/N0561218.pdf?OpenElement.
    November 17, 2005.

83. Gell, F.R. and Roberts, C.M. *The Fishery Effects of Marine
    Reserves and Fishery Closures.* Washington, D.C.: D.C.World
    Wildlife Fund, 2003.

84. World Wildlife Fund. "New report shows important benefits of
    marine reserve networks for fishing communities and oceans."
    Press Release. Available online. URL: http://worldwildlife.org/
    news/displayPR.cfm?prID=31. August 28, 2003.

85. The World Conservation Union. "Conserving biodiversity."
    Available online. URL: http://www.iucn.org/themes/wcpa/theme/
    conserving.html. 2005.

86. Environmental Protection Agency. Press Release, Region 3. Avail-
    able online. URL: www.delawareestuary.org. November 29, 2005.

FURTHER READING

Books

Carson, Rachel. *The Sea Around Us.* New York: Oxford University Press, 1952.

Ellis, Richard. *The Empty Ocean: Plundering the World's Marine Life.* Washington, D.C.: Island Press, 2003.

Fujita, Rod. *Heal the Ocean: Solutions for Saving Our Seas.* Gabriola, Canada: New Society Publishers, 2003.

Goodall, Jane. *Reason for Hope.* New York: Warner Books, 1999.

Pauly, Daniel and Jay Maclean. *In a Perfect Ocean: The State of Fisheries and Ecosystems in the North Atlantic Ocean.* Washington, DC: Island Press, 2002.

Web Sites

The Nature Conservancy
http://www.nature.org

The Ocean Conservancy
http://www.oceanconservancy.org

Pew Oceans Commission
http://www.pewoceans.org

The U.S. Commission on Ocean Policy
http://www.oceancommission.gov

World Wildlife Fund
http://www.worldwildlife.org

Wetlands

WHAT'S IN THE NEWS

Quite simply, wetlands are in the news because of their valuable services. Science continues to demonstrate that wetlands provide pollution abatement, improve water quality, contribute many billions of dollars to our economy in goods and services, and provide valuable habitat for important plants and animals. The news comes when we lose those wetland benefits—when flooding increases because of wetland loss, as with Hurricane Katrina, or when recreation areas are degraded or destroyed.

Wetlands are also in the news as people try to decide the best way to protect our remaining wetlands, while allowing for the inevitable development that comes from increasing population demands. To develop policies and regulations to protect wetlands, however, we have to agree on a definition. This question has drawn the attention of the Supreme Court.

The fact that wetlands are protected to a certain extent by regulations is good news, but wetlands continue to be under attack from many sources, such as air and water pollution, global warming, weakened regulations, and development.

THE SCIENCE

What Is a Wetland?

A wetland is defined by **hydrology** (the science of how water moves), soils, and vegetation. Wetlands are areas of land that are covered with water for certain periods of time each year. Land that is saturated with water leads to the development of certain types of soils and soil conditions, which then allows for the growth of particular plants.[1] A wetland, therefore, is generally defined as land that has (1) standing water for a certain period each year; (2) unique soil conditions that are different from those found in adjacent uplands; and (3) vegetation adapted to living in wet conditions.[2]

The hydrology, or the way in which water moves, affects the physical conditions and chemistry of an area. For example, flooded or saturated areas are low in oxygen, which slows decomposition of organic matter. Therefore, most wetland soils are largely made from organic matter, or decomposing plants and animals. In turn, only certain types of plants, for example cattails, are adapted to live in such soils and water conditions.

Because the surface of the Earth is not uniformly flat or wet, different types of wetlands exist. Marshes, **bogs**, **pocosins**, **muskegs**, swamps, salt marshes, and **prairie potholes** are all wetlands. Differences in the lay of the land, or topography, and the climate contribute to whether a forested wetland, such as a red maple or cypress swamp, a **vernal pool**, a marsh, or a **fen** will develop and be maintained. Each type of wetland has different plants, soils, and levels of water during the year.

The question of what constitutes a wetland is important because of federal regulations protecting our remaining wetlands. For regulatory purposes under the Clean Water Act, the term *wetlands* means the following:

> [T]hose areas that are inundated or saturated by surface or groundwater at a frequency and duration sufficient to support, and that under normal circumstances do support, a prevalence of vegetation typically adapted for life in saturated soil conditions. Wetlands generally include swamps, marshes, bogs and similar areas.[3]

Most states base their wetland delineation, or wetland boundaries, on the 1987 manual, *The Federal Manual for Identifying and Delineating Jurisdictional Wetlands*, adopted by the U.S. Environmental Protection Agency (EPA), the U.S. Army Corps of Engineers, the U.S. Fish and Wildlife Service (FWS), and the Natural Resources Conservation Service (NRCS).

Where Are Wetlands Found?

Wetlands can be found in places where water remains near the surface of the ground for extended periods of time. Some wetlands are ephemeral, such as vernal pools, and are wet for only a few weeks in the spring. Others, such as mangrove or maple swamps, are flooded with water most of the year. Wetlands are found in the northern tundra, along the ocean's edge, in old glacial lake beds, and along river floodplains. In fact, wetlands are found on every continent except Antarctica.

The majority of wetlands found in the United States, about 80 percent, are inland wetlands: forested wetlands, marshes, and bogs are examples. The remaining 20 percent of our wetlands are found along low-lying coastal areas, where waters from the ocean tides mix with freshwater from the land to create brackish water. Examples of these coastal wetlands include salt marshes, tidal marshes, and mangrove swamps.[4]

How Do Wetlands Form?

Wetlands form in areas where water collects—whether in a mountain meadow fed by snowmelt, a fen fed by groundwater, or a salt marsh fed by streams and the ocean tides. Wetlands are transition areas between land and water. Several conditions determine if a wetland will form in a particular area: the hydrology, the climate, the geology, and the topography (the lay of the land).

The hydrology, or the way the water moves, is a key to how a wetland forms and how it functions (Figure 2.1). A wetland needs to have more water coming in than leaving for at least certain parts of the year. Water enters a wetland through precipitation, groundwater, or surface water (rivers, lakes, or the ocean). Water leaves a wetland through evaporation from the ground surface or from plants. Water also leaves when surface water or groundwater flows out of the system. As one might expect, areas of the country with climates of higher rainfall and lower evaporation, such as the East Coast and the Northwestern United States have more wetlands than the desert climates of the Southwest.

The hydrology of an area changes with the seasons or with human water use. For example, groundwater or rivers usually supply water to wetlands. At drier times of the year, or if water has been pumped from the ground or the nearby river, a wetland may recharge, or contribute, water to the ground or the surface water.

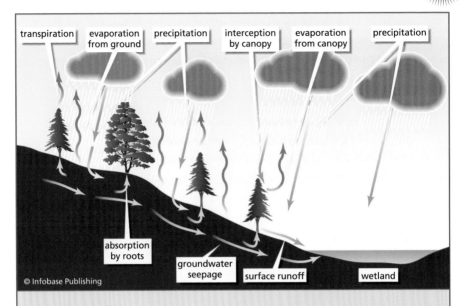

Figure 2.1 Wetlands form in areas in which water collects, creating conditions that develop hydric soils and allow plants adapted to the soil and water conditions to grow.

The hydrology of an area is also shaped by the geology and the topography. For example, as the last glaciers melted about 14,000 years ago, they scraped out many depressions and left areas filled with water. The Great Lakes and their wetlands were formed in this way, as were the prairie pothole marshes in the Midwest and the many glacial lakes and associated wetlands in the northeastern United States. Wetlands can also form over long periods of time as lakes or ponds fill with sediment from eroding rock or accumulating organic matter.

What Are the Different Types of Wetlands?

Coastal Wetlands

Wetlands are areas that create a transition zone between land and water. Coastal wetlands are low-lying areas that receive water from both the twice-daily ocean tides and the freshwater from streams or rivers. The water in a coastal wetland varies in salinity levels depending on time of day and the amount of freshwater mixing. Coastal wetlands include salt marshes, tidal freshwater marshes, and mangrove swamps.

Salt Marshes

A salt marsh is a balancing act (Figure 2.2). These marshes develop where enough sediment accumulates to support the salt grasses and rushes that, in turn, trap the sediment, or soils, to build a marsh. In a salt marsh, sediment accumulation is balanced against the forces of land subsiding, ocean scouring, and sea-level rising. Salt marshes are found along protected coasts at middle and high latitudes and are most common along the eastern United States.

Figure 2.2 A salt marsh in Acadia National Park, Maine. Salt marshes develop in coastal areas where enough sediment accumulates to support plants that are adapted to the daily mixing of fresh and salt water.

Salt marshes are one of the most productive ecosystems in the world.[5] They export organic matter with the outgoing tides and, thus, provide a huge energy input into the ocean ecosystem. Much of the energy flow in the marsh is accomplished by bacteria or fungi that use sulfur instead of oxygen. These **anaerobic** processes give salt marshes their distinct hydrogen sulfide (rotten eggs) smell.

Tidal Freshwater Marshes

Tidal freshwater marshes share characteristics with both salt marshes and freshwater inland marshes. Tidal marshes are found further inland, but still receive tidal flushing. They have a high diversity of plants and are used by more birds than any other type of marsh.[6] The plants benefit from the nutrients brought in with the tides without having to experience the high-salt stress environment because of their location.

Mangrove Swamps

In the United States, mangrove swamps are found from southern Florida to Puerto Rico. The mangrove tree has adapted to living in a saline, or salty, environment by growing prop roots, having roots that keep salt from entering, and producing live seedlings (Figure 2.3). Mangrove swamps provide organic matter to surrounding coastal areas, buffer the shore from hurricanes, and provide homes to a diversity of animal species.[7] In addition, mangrove wetlands are important as nursery areas for fish and as food sources for commercial and sport fish.

Inland Wetlands

Inland Freshwater Marshes

From one-acre prairie potholes to the largest freshwater marsh in the United States—the Florida Everglades—inland freshwater marshes form a diverse group of wetlands. All are freshwater ecosystems filled with grasses, sedges, and other wetland emergent plants.

Prairie potholes were formed in depressions left by melting glaciers, more than 10,000 years ago, in what is today Minnesota,

Figure 2.3 A Mangrove swamp in Trinidad. Mangrove swamps are important nursery areas for many species of fish and provide a shoreline buffer from hurricanes.

the Dakotas, Iowa, and into bordering Canada. These small wetlands provide valuable habitats for birds, yet more than half have been drained to provide more land for agriculture. The Everglades in Florida is a unique wetland system, dominated by saw grass marshes. It is home to more than 300 species of birds and more than 15 endangered and threatened animal species.

Inland freshwater marshes are also found along lakes and rivers. Vegetation varies, but dominant marsh plants can include different species of cattails, juncuses, sedges, wild rice, bur weed, and bulrushes. Many mammals visit marshes to feed, and marshes are home to an abundance of birds because of the rich food supply and excellent nesting sites. Amphibians—frogs, toads, and salamanders—are also an important animal group found in marshes. They eat insects and are, in turn, an important food source for the birds, mammals, and fish of the marshes.

Peatlands

Peatlands is a term used to describe bogs and fens, special wetlands that form in cool, northern areas (Figure 2.4). Peatlands form only when more water stays on the ground than evaporates. Under certain conditions, excess water causes peat (partially decomposed sphagnum moss) to accumulate. Bogs are acidic and poor in nutrients, so bog plants have special adaptations. Some, such as the carnivorous pitcher and sundew plants, have adapted to the nutrient-poor conditions by capturing and digesting insects. Fens, usually fed by groundwater, have more minerals and, therefore, more variety of plant species.

Figure 2.4 A peatland in Maine. Peatlands (bogs and fens) provide important wetland functions, such as wildlife habitat and biodiversity.

Forested Wetlands

Forested wetlands, sometimes called swamps, are found throughout the United States. Cypress swamps are found in the Southeast in deep water (Figure 2.5). Atlantic white cedar and red maple swamps are found in the eastern United States. Forested wetlands are also found throughout the Midwest, filling the basins or ponds left by the last glacier. As in all wetlands, many organisms feed on the decomposing organic matter, or detritus. These invertebrates, such as snails, clams, and worms, in turn, serve as food for the mammals, amphibians, reptiles, and birds of the forest. Forested wetlands provide important habitat to many species of animals and plants.

Riparian Wetlands

Riparian wetlands form along rivers and streams (Figure 2.6). The soils and plants that grow in these wetlands are influenced

Figure 2.5 This cypress swamp in Georgia is an example of a forested wetland. The cypress is one of only a few types of trees that are adapted to live in continuously flooded areas.

Figure 2.6   An example of a riparian wetland is this floodplain of the Penobscot River in Maine. Riparian wetlands provide valuable habitat between the river and the upland.

by what is carried downstream—sediment, water, nutrients, and even pollution. Bottomwood hardwood (or floodplain) forests are often extensive riparian wetlands found in the eastern and southern parts of the United States. The ivory-billed woodpecker, a bird long thought extinct, was found recently in just such a riparian forest in Arkansas. In the western United States, riparian areas exist as much narrower bands found along streams winding through steep terrain.

Riparian wetlands create "edge" habitats, areas between the river and the upland. These areas are notably rich in biological productivity, and riparian areas are even more productive because of the water and nutrients provided by periodic flooding. E.P. Odum noted that a riparian zone is "an interface between man's most vital resource, namely, water, and his living space, the land."[8]

Why Are Wetlands Important?

Wetlands serve many functions, both ecological and economic. Not all wetlands are the same type or size, and, therefore, they do not all play the same ecological role. However, in general, wetlands (1) store water much like a sponge, which prevents flooding, recharges groundwater, and increases water quality; (2) cycle nutrients and energy; and (3) create habitats for plants and animals. This broad range of functions gives wetlands huge economic value to humans. Not until the 1970s, however, did scientists and conservationists began to speak in terms of "wetland values."[9]

Wetlands are extremely valuable in various arenas. On one level, plants and animals depend on wetlands for places to find food and shelter. Wetlands are critical links to larger ecosystems. Wetlands also play an important role on a global level.[10]

Habitat and Recreational Use

Wetlands provide critical habitat for many species of birds and amphibians that use them for food, shelter, and breeding. In addition, many mammals, fish, and reptiles use various wetlands for food or shelter. Among these inhabitants are more than 100 animal species that are listed as endangered.[11] Wetlands are some of the most biologically productive ecosystems on our planet.[12] In many wetlands, the nutrient-rich environment supports plants or decomposing matter that provide the base of a food chain that feeds fish, birds, and mammals. In addition, although wetlands occupy only 3.5 percent of our land, they contain 31 percent of our plant species.[13]

An economic value is hard to place on the habitat function of wetlands, but some figures give a sense of their monetary significance. A 2003 U.S. Fish and Wildlife report, "The National Survey of Fishing, Hunting, and Wildlife-Associated Recreation," states that people who watch birds in the United States, all 46 million of them, spent about $32 billion on gear and related expenses. Of note is that 68 percent of those people watched birds around lakes or streamside areas (wetlands).[14] The money spent on birding generated an additional $85 billion in economic benefits, produced

$13 billion in taxes, and created more than 800,000 jobs. Waterfowl hunters spent almost $1 billion in 2001 on equipment and for other expenses.[15] Sportfishing generated $36 billion in 2001 (Figure 2.7). One study found that an estimated $79 billion a year from commercial and recreational fishing is generated by wetland-dependent species—approximately 70 percent of the entire fishing industry.[16] If shellfish species are included, the percentage of wetland-dependent species increases to 95 percent.

Environmental Quality Indicator

A group of wetland residents acts as a "miner's canary" by letting us know when an environmental problem exists. Because of their porous skin, amphibians, such frogs, toads, and salamanders, act

Figure 2.7 Fly-fishing on the Little River in the Great Smoky Mountains is a popular leisure activity. The Great Smoky Mountains is a mountain range straddling the border between Tennessee and North Carolina, where hiking, sightseeing, and fishing are the main tourist attractions.

as little environmental sponges, absorbing pollution and ultraviolet rays more easily than creatures with hair, scale, or fur. Just as the miner's canary that died in mines filled with poisonous gas that humans could not detect, amphibians are a biological indicator of problems. Today's amphibians are in danger from many directions—pollution, global warming, **ozone** depletion, habitat loss—and the message to many scientists is that wetlands are likewise threatened.

Water Quality
Wetlands improve water quality in several ways. Wetlands slow the flow of water as it becomes trapped in sediment and around plants. When water is not moving, sediment settles out of the water, while also allowing time for chemical and biological processes to remove bacteria and pollutants.

Flood Reduction/Groundwater Recharge
Because wetlands can absorb large amounts of water, like a sponge, they are key landscape features in preventing flooding. Surges of water are absorbed and slowly released over time, either into nearby streams and lakes or into groundwater. In times when water flow is low because of the season, or because of humans diverting water flow, wetlands serve the opposite function and release water into nearby streams and lakes or into the groundwater.

As an example, the U.S. Army Corps of Engineers estimated that wetland protection along the Charles River in Massachusetts saved about $17 million in potential flood damage.[17] An acre of wetland is estimated to store between 1 million gallons (3.7 million liters) and 1.5 million gallons (5.6 million L) of floodwater. In the early 1990s, flooding in the upper Mississippi River basin caused about $20 billion in damage. The historic loss of wetlands around the river increased the severity of the flooding and damages.[18] As Hurricane Katrina taught the country in September of 2005, the destruction of more than 1,900 square miles (4,920 sq km) of wetlands since 1930 has left the area more susceptible to hurricane damage.

Global Importance

As scientists continue to learn how ecosystems interact, they appreciate the role of wetlands in such global issues as air quality, ocean health, and the cycling of carbon dioxide and methane, both greenhouse gases.

What Are the Threats to Wetlands?

Development

The United States currently loses about 60,000 acres (242.8 sq km) of wetlands a year, and the largest single cause of that loss is land filled or drained for development.[19] Our expanding population means a continually increased need for homes, industry, roads, and other services.

Water Use: Changes in Hydrology

Streams, lakes, groundwater, and precipitation can supply the water necessary to sustain wetlands. When humans divert the streams or pump water from the lakes or ground, wetlands lose water. Over time, the decrease in the water flow can damage or destroy the wetlands.

Another change in water flow that destroys wetlands is caused by damming rivers to create reservoirs. As the river water fills the reservoir, wetlands along the former river are drowned. In addition, the wetlands downstream of the dam are deprived of both water and sediment the river had previously supplied. Water flow also changes as riverbeds are dredged or channeled, a common practice in this country for many years. In Louisiana, before Hurricane Katrina in 2005, these human-made changes all contributed to the loss of significant portions of coastal wetlands each year.

Pollution

As any sponge can hold only so much water, the amount of pollution a wetland can absorb or treat has a limit. Human activities degrade wetlands in many ways: accumulation of sediment, heavy metals, road salts, pesticides, and petroleum products,

Figure 2.8 In this aerial shot, nonpoint pollution runs via the Nemadji River into Lake Superior. Erosional run-off caused by heavy rains can be seen in this image as well.

for example. The EPA has stated that nonpoint source pollution, such as runoff from roads, parking lots, and agricultural operations, is the single largest pollutant of water.[20] In addition, what pollutes surface waters also pollutes the connected wetlands (Figure 2.8).

Invasive Species/Grazing

Invasive species are plants and animals that are not native, or indigenous, to an ecosystem. Invasive plants can crowd out native plants that local animals need for food and shelter. Invasive animals can eat the food of, take over the shelter from, or even eat the local animals. The EPA considers invasive species to be one of the largest threats to our terrestrial, coastal, and freshwater ecosystems.[21] Invasive species cause billions of dollars in damage in various ecosystems, and wetlands have not escaped this damage. An example is purple loosestrife (*Lythrum salicaria*), a tall plant with purple flowers that aggressively crowds out native marsh plants needed by wetland animals to survive. Water hyacinth and zebra mussels are other invasive species that cause large economic and environmental damage, including loss of native species, changes in water levels, and detrimental effects on recreational and commercial activities.

Invasive species can come from ballast water, the water carried in hulls of ships from all over the world, and these species can be released after the ships arrive in the United States. They can also be introduced accidentally or intentionally by humans. For example, bullfrogs released in a marsh or stream can cause severe damage to a local wetland by eating large numbers of native fish, insects, and even small mammals, snakes, and birds.

Global Warming

The predictions of many scientists, including the Intergovernmental Panel on Climate Change, are that global temperatures are increasing and the icecaps are melting.[22] What does this situation mean for wetlands? With possible sea-level rises from 4–35 inches (10.1–88.9 cm), many coastal wetlands will flood. In addition, as global climate patterns shift, the precipitation patterns will change water levels and cause the loss of some inland wetlands. Shifting climate patterns are already causing changes in both plant and animal reproductive strategies, as changes in food or shelter availability disrupt typical patterns.

Global warming, therefore, will directly affect the way many wetlands function because of shifts in water availability and flow. Climate changes will also affect the plants and animals that live in wetlands.

Agricultural Lands

From the mid-1950s until the mid-1970s, 87 percent of wetlands loss was a result of filling the wetlands to form new agricultural land. Government policy encouraged farmers to fill, or "reclaim," wetlands. Today, legislation prevents such widespread conversions.

HISTORY OF THE ISSUE

Wetland Loss

The term *wetland* was not commonly used before the middle of the twentieth century.[23] Before that time, people called them bogs, marshes, moors, or swamps. The area that was to become the continental United States had approximately 221 million acres (894,355 sq km) of wetlands in the early 1600s (about the size of Texas and Utah combined).[24] People viewed these areas as wastelands to be reclaimed and made useful for farming and development. In fact, government policy subsidized people in their efforts to destroy wetlands. Until 1985, wetlands on agricultural land and commercial forests were exempt from protection of Section 404 of the Clean Water Act.

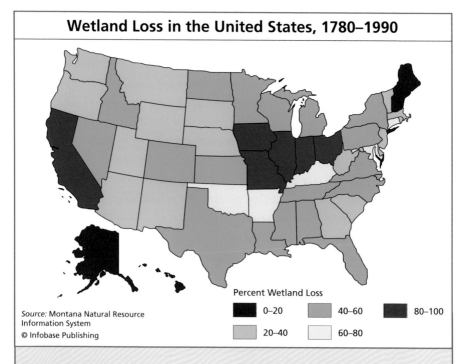

Wetland Loss in the United States, 1780–1990

Percent Wetland Loss

0–20 40–60 80–100

20–40 60–80

Source: Montana Natural Resource Information System
© Infobase Publishing

Figure 2.9 Over the last 200 years, wetlands have been disappearing in the United States at an alarming rate.

As a result, by the 1980s, only half of America's original wetlands remained (Figure 2.9). Six states had destroyed 85 percent of their wetlands, and 22 states had destroyed 50 percent or more.[25] River floodplains, bottom-land forests, and coastal plains contained rich organic soils that, once drained, can become productive farmlands. Wetland forests were logged to meet the lumber demands of a growing population. Wetlands were also destroyed in other ways. America's history records the construction of hundreds of dams by the U.S. Army Corps of Engineers. Building a dam floods, and therefore destroys, the wetlands of the associated rivers.

Estimates for wetland loss in the continental United States from the mid-1970s to the mid-1980s are approximately 290,000 acres (1,173.5 sq km) per year.[26] The U.S. Fish and Wildlife Service estimates that the loss of wetlands between 1986 and 1997 slowed to about 60,000 acres (242.8 sq km) per year.[27]

Yet a definite number is hard to determine, as wetlands are lost not only through filling and draining but also through the effects of pollution, water diversion for development purposes, and other causes.

Wetland Policy and Regulations

In the 1800s, the United States appeared to be an endless bounty of natural resources. As the population grew, the federal government passed laws and developed policies to facilitate the settling of new lands. One such law was the Swamp Land Act of 1849, which gave certain states the jurisdiction to reclaim, or drain, swamplands.[28] Another example was the 1905 U.S. Bureau of Reclamation Klamath Reclamation Project, designed to drain the lakes and marshes around the Lower Klamath and Tule Lake in the Pacific Northwest. The drained land was used for agriculture and development. Today, with less than 25 percent of the original wetlands left, the area is the object of heated controversy and lawsuits, as the agriculture interests battle the environmental concerns for use of the water—agriculture versus habitat.

In the 1970s, a policy shift occurred that reflected a scientific understanding of the many functions and values of wetlands. This shift was clearly represented in the new regulations to protect what remained of America's wetlands.

To protect something, however, people must agree on what that something is. Is a wetland wet all the time? Do cattails have to grow there? Does a wetland have to have a thick peat soil? In search of a legal definition, the U.S. Fish and Wildlife Service published a report in 1979 that defined wetlands on the basis of water, vegetation, and soils. The primary goal of the wetland classification, according to the report, "is to impose boundaries on natural ecosystems for the purpose of inventory, evaluation, and management."[29]

Wetlands are currently protected under Section 404 of the 1972 Clean Water Act, which states that wetlands cannot be filled or destroyed without a permit from the U.S. Army Corps of Engineers. Initially, the regulation was narrowly interpreted to include only navigable waters, but two court cases in 1974 and 1975, and an Executive Order, caused the Corps of Engineers to broaden its interpretation:

> . . . environmentally vital areas, [wetlands] constitute a productive and valuable public resource, the unnecessary alteration or destruction of which should be discouraged as contrary to the public interest (Federal Register, July 25, 1975).

The permits are issued after consideration of many factors—such as conservation, economics, aesthetics, and water issues.[30]

Coastal wetlands, such as tidal marshes and salt marshes, are protected under the 1972 Coastal Zone Management Act. The Act provides financial incentives and technical support to the eligible 35 states (including the Great Lakes states) and territories to develop voluntary Coastal Zone Management Plans. The 1982 Coastal Barrier Resource Act denies federal monies to development within undeveloped, unprotected coastal barrier systems, which includes wetlands.[31]

In 1985, the government passed a "Swamp Buster" law, which makes farmers who drained their land for agricultural purposes no longer eligible for most federal farm subsidies. Two years later, at the request of the U.S. Environmental Protection Agency, the National Wetlands Policy Forum developed a plan that included what was to become the catchphrase of American wetland policy:

> [T]o achieve no overall net loss of the nation's remaining wetlands base and to create and restore wetlands, where feasible, to increase the quantity and quality of the nation's wetland resource base.[32]

Thus, the phrase "no net loss" became a part of President George H.W. Bush's environmental policy. To be realistic, the goal could not be the preservation of all existing wetlands. Rather, it became the policy that any wetland permitted for destruction must be replaced in some other location to ensure "no net loss." Wetland **mitigation**, as it is called, is a subject of continued debate as the success of artificial wetlands, or trading one wetland type for another, is called into question by scientists and some policymakers.

CURRENT ISSUES AND FUTURE CONSIDERATIONS

Wetland Regulation

Since the 1970s, Section 404 of the Clean Water Act has provided some measure of protection for wetlands, as evidenced by the decrease in wetland loss. Scientific reports, however, including a 2001 report by the National Academies, are finding that the Clean Water Action Section 404 needs to be improved to achieve the goal of "no net loss" of wetlands.[33]

Federal regulatory issues still include refining the legal definition of wetlands. For example, does a wetland that is near, or adjacent to, a waterway receive protection? In October of 2005, the United States Supreme Court agreed to hear two cases that deal with wetlands without obvious connection to "navigable waterways." The wetlands are in some manner adjacent or next to a waterway. The first case, *Rapanos v. United States,* involves the clearing and filling of land that, although not adjacent to, does drain into a "navigable waterway." Lower courts found that the filling was prohibited by the Clean Water Act.

The second case, *Carabell v. Army Corps of Engineers*, deals with a wetland separated from "navigable waters" by a human-made berm, one that is at times hydrologically (by ground or surface water) connected to a "navigable waterway." Lower courts determined the area was a wetland falling under federal jurisdiction.

In June 2006, the U.S. Supreme Court sided with Mr. Rapanos in ruling that isolated wetlands could not be regulated under Section 404 of the Clean Water Act. However, the Court was deeply divided on the issue, and states and cities are not clear on how the ruling should be interpreted at these levels. It may be that after this ruling, state and local governments may choose to pass their own regulations. This pattern is already evident in the area of clean air and global climate-change regulations, with many states and cities passing stronger regulations to address perceived weaknesses in Federal regulations. Such variability in regulations makes doing business in more than one state difficult for some companies.

Wetland Mitigation

Wetland mitigation, or building a new wetland to offset the permitted filling of an existing wetland, is not as straightforward a solution to "no net loss" as it may appear. For one thing, not all wetlands are created equal—some have more habitat, water quality, or flood control value than others. Wetland value depends on many factors, including the landscape, size, wetland type, and connection to surface water and groundwater. A 2006 report released by the U.S. Fish and Wildlife Service has raised doubts about what the government is calling "no net loss."[34] The concern is that the government report made no assessment as to the quality of the remaining wetlands. Many scientists would argue that a golf course pond does not have the same wetland value as a salt marsh or a bog.

Trying to construct new wetlands is also complicated by the fact that wetland systems are complex—one cannot simply flood an area and get a wetland of comparable value or even be assured the wetland that will survive. Some forested wetlands (swamps), for example, may take hundreds of years to develop. Whereas salt marshes have been successfully recreated, certain ecosystems, such as vernal pools, bogs, and fens, have proved impossible to create.[35]

Yet another issue is maintaining the wetland. If mitigation plans include diverting water to create a marsh area, what happens when the water supply is ended five years later because an adjacent landowner decides to exercise water rights and withdraw most of the water? Studies have shown that created wetlands are more likely to fail than restored wetlands.[36,37]

A report issued in 2001 by the National Academies of Science provided a summary that highlights the problems involved in recreating wetlands and monitoring the outcome of the projects:

> In conclusion, the literature and long-term trajectories reported therein suggest that wetland restoration and creation sites do not often achieve functional equivalency with reference sites within 5 years; indeed, up to 20 years may be needed for functional attributes to be determined or assessed correctly.[38]

In addition, the report concludes that the expectations of Section 404 are often unclear, and compliance is often not achieved. Their conclusion, based on 20 years of data, clearly states that the goal of "no net loss" of wetlands is not being met by wetland mitigation programs.[39]

Mitigation Banks

A federal program was developed in 1995 to give policy and procedural guidance to state and federal agencies trying to develop wetland mitigation banks. The program is similar to one where industries buy and sell clean air credits as a means of decreasing air pollution. The idea of a mitigation bank was written to mean the following:

> [A] site where wetlands and/or other aquatic resources are restored, created, enhanced, or in exceptional circumstances, preserved,

expressly for the purpose of providing compensatory mitigation in advance of authorized impacts to similar resources.[40]

For example, if a wetlands permit allows for the filling of five acres of wetlands, the developer would have the mitigation option of purchasing existing wetlands at another site instead of trying to build a new wetland. Developers could also sell wetland credits to the bank if their project site has undisturbed wetlands.

Nevertheless, a need to improve and refine the practices of site selection, design, implementation, monitoring, and long-term management for all compensatory mitigation projects, including mitigation banks, continues to exist. A 2006 study by two legal experts titled, "The Effects of Wetland Mitigation Banking on People" concluded that wetland mitigation banking redistributes wetland resources from urban areas to rural areas and leaves city dwellers with fewer important environmental services, such as water filtration, **erosion** protection, and flood control.[41]

As scientists continue to collect data, the debate continues as to whether mitigation banks will provide more success than other programs. The 2001 National Academies of Science Report on wetland mitigation concluded, "Third-party compensation approaches (mitigation banks, in-lieu fee programs) offer some advantages over permittee-responsible mitigation."[42] In other words, no one has easy answers yet as to how to compensate for wetlands that are destroyed because of development.

Programs and Policies to Protect Wetlands

Many programs and government policies work toward protecting and improving the quality of existing wetlands. Government and private groups pool resources and expertise to provide funding to protect land, educate the public, and improve water quality. In addition, the quality of the air, the upland areas, and global climate change all have an impact on the quality of wetlands and the species living in them. Therefore, any program or policy that addresses air quality, global warming, or pollution of land also helps protect wetlands.

Since wetlands are formed by water, both the quality of the water and the quantity of available water affect them. The EPA has stated that nonpoint source pollution is the largest source of water pollution today.[43] Thus, programs to decrease nonpoint source pollution also help to improve the quality of wetlands. Because wetlands are low-lying areas that are connected to other areas in the landscape, it often happens that water, pollution, and sediment end up in a wetland. Therefore, the EPA has incorporated a "watershed-based" approach to water and wetland protection.[44] A watershed, or drainage area, is the area from which all water and sediment flows into a river, lake, ocean, or other body of water. The EPA is actively pursuing an integrated approach to watershed management by providing funding and technical assistance to help states with watershed and wetlands planning projects.

Another consideration in wetland protection is that about 74 percent of our nation's remaining wetlands are on private lands.[45] Voluntary protection programs become a key part of wetland protection. One such incentive for private landowners is a Natural Resources Conservation Service (NRCS) program called the Wetland Reserve Program.[46] The program is designed to offer technical and financial support to private landowners so that they can maintain the highest wetland functions and values for their sites.

In addition, partnerships among private, government, and public organizations provide the resources to attack larger preservation or restoration projects. Ducks Unlimited (DU), a private organization, has been working for the past 60 years to protect wetlands around the country and around the world. They have contributed to the conservation of more than 9.4 million acres of habitat for migratory birds.[47] Ducks Unlimited supports and funds projects on private lands that meet the goals of the North American Waterfowl Management Plan. In addition, Ducks Unlimited partners with state and local governments, private landowners, and conservation organizations to purchase wetlands.

Another example of such a partnership is the Great Shorelines Preserve along the Great Salt Lake in Utah. The Preserve protects about 4,000 acres (16.1 sq km) of wetlands along the Great Salt Lake, a major migratory flyway for about 6 million birds a year and a Western Hemisphere Shorebird Reserve. In addition, the Everglades is the site for a major collaborative effort among state and federal agencies. In 2000, the United States government undertook an $8 billion, 50-year restoration plan that draws on both state and federal funds. The Comprehensive Everglades Restoration Project (CERP) was developed in recognition of the inestimable ecological importance of the Everglades, the largest freshwater marsh in the United States. The Everglades is also a national park designated as a world heritage site (1979), an international biosphere reserve (1976), and a Ramsar wetland of international importance (1987).

Wetlands are also an international resource. In 1986, Canada and the United States formed a partnership (which Mexico joined in 1994) called the North American Waterfowl Management Plan, to restore waterfowl populations through habitat protection, restoration, and enhancement. Waterfowl live, feed, and breed in wetlands. They are the most economically important group of migratory birds on our continent. By 2003, the member countries had invested more than $3.2 billion toward habitat protection and restoration, which affected more than 13.1 million acres of habitat (an area about the size of Delaware).

WHAT THE INDIVIDUAL CAN DO

Concerned citizens can help preserve the wetlands in a number of ways:

* Encourage your state and local governments to pass regulations that protect wetlands and their watersheds.
* Become involved in some type of watershed/river/ lake volunteer monitoring program. Details may be available from local conservation groups or your state department of environmental protection. If none exists, you may be able to begin a program, modeled after the many successful citizen monitoring

programs around the country (for example, The University of Rhode Island's Watershed Watch Program).

✳ If you have wetlands on your property, take measures to protect them or enhance their value. Keep a buffer strip of natural vegetation between the lawn and the wetland to filter out pollutants. In New England, participate in the EPA's "Adopt a Wetland" program.

✳ Minimize your use of pesticides, herbicides, and fertilizers. Even if you do not live near a wetland, these materials contribute to nonpoint source pollution and eventually may end up in storm drains, rivers, and wetlands.

REFERENCES

1. Cowardin, L.M., et al. *Classification of Wetlands and Deepwater Habitats of the United States.* Washington DC: U.S. Fish and Wildlife Service, 1979.
2. Mitsch, William J. and James G. Gosselink. *Wetlands.* Hoboken, N.J.: John Wiley & Sons, 2000.
3. U.S. Environmental Protection Agency. "Wetlands definitions: 40 CFR 230.3(t) Clean Water Act," Available online. URL: http://www.epa.gov/owow/wetlands/what/definitions.html.
4. Mitsch and Gosselink, *Wetlands*, p. 72.
5. Ibid., p. 261
6. Idid., p.307
7. Ibid., p. 256
8. Ibid., p. 514
9. Novitzki, Richard P., et al. "United States Geological Survey. Water supply paper 242: National water summary on wetland resources restoration, creation, and recovery of wetlands," Available online. URL: http://water.usgs.gov/nwsum/WSP2425/functions.html.
10. Mitsch and Gosselink, *Wetlands*, p. 591.
11. Ibid., p. 583
12. Tiner, R.W. "Wetlands of Rhode Island," Newton Corner, Mass: U.S. Fish and Wildlife Service, 1989. Available online. URL: http://water.usgs.gov/nwsum/WSP2425/history.html.
13. "Functions and values of wetlands," U.S. EPA 843-F-01-002c. Available online, URL: www.epa.gov/watertrain/wetlands/. 2001.
14. La Rouch, Genevieve. "Birding in the US: A demographic and economic analysis. Addendum," U.S. Fish and Wildlife. Available online. URL: http://library.fws.gov/nat_survey2001_birding.pdf. 2003.
15. Ibid.
16. "Functions and values of wetlands," U.S. EPA 843-F-01-002c. Available online. URL: www.epa.gov/watertrain/wetlands/. 2001.
17. La Rouch, Genevieve. "Birding in the U.S.: A demographic and economic analysis. Addendum," U.S. Fish and Wildlife. Available online. URL: http://library.fws.gov/nat_survey2001_birding.pdf. 2003.
18. Kolva, James R. "National water summary on wetland resources. Restoration, creation, and recovery of wetlands: Effects of the

Great Midwest Flood of 1993 on wetlands," United States Geological Survey Water Supply Paper 2425. Available online. URL: http://water.usgs.gov/nwsum/WSP2425/flood.html.

19. U.S. Environmental Protection Agency. "Threats to wetlands: What is the status of our nation's wetlands?" Available online. URL:www.epa.gov/owow/wetlands/facts/threats.pdf. 2001

20. U.S. Environmental Protection Agency. "Factsheet: Nonpoint source pollution," EPA841-F-96-004A. Available online. URL: http://www.epa.gov/owow/nps/facts/point1.htm. 2006.

21. U.S. Environmental Protection Agency. "Invasive species." Available online. URL: http://www.epa.gov/owow/invasive_species/. 2005.

22. Intergovernmental Panel on Climate Change. "IPCC third assessment report: Climate change 2001: Synthesis report: Summary for policymakers." Available online. URL: http://www.ipcc.ch/pub/un/syreng/spm.pdf.

23. Mitsch and Gosselink, *Wetlands*, p. 25.

24. Dahl, T.E., and Johnson, C.E. *Wetlands—Status and Trends in the Conterminous United States, Mid-1970's to Mid-1980's*. Washington, D.C.: U.S. Fish and Wildlife Service, 1991.

25. Dahl, T.E. *Wetlands—Losses in the United States, 1780's to 1980's*. Washington, DC: U.S. Fish and Wildlife Service, 1990.

26. Dahl, Thomas E. and Allord, Gregory J. "Technical aspect of wetlands. national water summary on wetland resources," United States Geological Survey Water Supply Paper 2425. Available online. URL: http://water.usgs.gov/nwsum/WSP2425/history.html.

27. National Research Council. *Compensating for Wetland Losses Under the Clean Water Act*. Washington, D.C.: National Academy Press, 2001.

28. Dahl, Thomas E. and Allord, Gregory J. "Technical aspect of wetlands. national water summary on wetland resources," United States Geological Survey Water Supply Paper 2425. Available online. URL: http://water.usgs.gov/nwsum/WSP2425/history.html.

29. Cowardin, et al., *Classification of Wetlands and Deepwater Habitats of the United States*.

30. Mitsch and Gosselink, *Wetlands*, p. 644.

31. Vottler, Todd H. and Muir, Thomas A. "National water summary on wetland resources, wetland management and research wetland

protection legislation," United States Geological Survey Water Supply Paper 2425. Available online: http://water.usgs.gov/nwsum/ WSP2425/legislation.html.

32. Mitsch and Gosselink, *Wetlands*, p. 642.

33. National Research Council. *Compensating for Wetland Losses Under the Clean Water Act*. Washington, D.C.: National Academy Press, 2001.

34. Barringer, Felcity. "Fewer marshes + more manmade ponds = increased wetlands," The *New York Times*. Available online. URL: http://select.nytimes.com/gst/abstract.html?res=FA0B10FD39540C 728FDDAA0894DE404482. March 31, 2006.

35. National Research Council. *Compensating for Wetland Losses Under the Clean Water Act*. Washington, D.C.: National Academy Press. 2001.

36. Kusler, J.A. and Kentula, M.E. *Wetland Creation and Restoration: The Status of the Science. Vol. 1 Regional Review*, Corvallis, Or: U.S. Environmental Protection Agency, Environmental Research Lab, 1989.

37. Mitsch, W.J. and Wilson, R.F. "Improving the success of wetland creation and restoration with know-how, time, and self-design." *Ecological Applications* 6 (1996): 77–83.

38. National Research Council, *Compensating for Wetland Losses Under the Clean Water Act*, p. 45.

39. Ibid., p. 2.

40. Mitsch and Gosselink, *Wetlands*, p. 685.

41. Ruhl, J.B. and Salzman, James E., "The effects of wetland mitigation banking on people," FSU College of Law, Public Law Research Paper No. 179. Available online. URL: http://ssrn.com/ abstract=878331. 2006

42. National Research Council, *Compensating for Wetland Losses Under the Clean Water Act*, p. 9.

43. U.S. Environmental Protection Agency. "Factsheet: Nonpoint source pollution," EPA841-F-96-004A. Available online. URL: http://www.epa.gov/owow/nps/facts/point1.htm. 2006.

44. U.S. Environmental Protection Agency. "Factsheet: Wetlands and watersheds," U.S. EPA. Available online. URL: http://www.epa.gov/ owow/wetlands/facts/fact26.html. 2005

45. Vottler and Muir, *National Water Summary on Wetland Resources Wetland Management and Research Wetland Protection Legislation.*

46. U.S. Environmental Protection Agency. "Mitigation banking: Compensating for impacts to wetlands and streams." Available online. URL: http://www.epa.gov/owow/wetlands/facts/fact16. html. 2005.

47. Ducks Unlimited. "Leaders in conservation factsheet." Available online. URL: http://www.ducks.org/about/faq/faq_conservation. asp#Difference. 2005.

FURTHER READING

Books

Goodall, Jane. *Reason for Hope.* New York: Warner Books. 1999.

Hardy, John T. *Climate Change: Causes, Effects, and Solutions.* Hoboken, N.J.: John Wiley & Sons, 2003.

Mitsch, William J. and Gosselink, James G. *Wetlands.* Hoboken, N.J.: John Wiley & Sons, 2000.

Odum, Eugene P. and Barrett, Gary W. *Fundamentals of Ecology.* Belmont, Calif.: Thomson Publishing, 2005.

Tiner, Ralph W. *In Search of Swampland: A Wetland Sourcebook and Field Guide.* Piscataway, N.J.: Rutgers University Press, 2005.

Web Sites

Wetland Mitigation

http://www.epa.gov/owow/wetlands/wetlandsmitigation/

http://water.usgs.gov/nwsum/WSP2425/restoration.html

Wetlands and Watersheds

http://water.usgs.gov/nwsum/WSP2425/

http://www.epa.gov/OWOW/

Wetlands Conservation/restoration Programs

http://www.nature.org/initiatives/freshwater/

http://www.nrcs.usda.gov/programs/wrp/

http://www.epa.gov/owow/wetlands/restore/5star/

Drinking Water

WHAT'S IN THE NEWS

We all need clean water to drink. One out of every six people in the world lacks access to clean drinking water. Although most of the people in the United States have access to clean water, some of America's drinking water is contaminated. Polluted water is in the news because it can cause serious health problems for people and destroy habitats. In addition, polluted water can cost millions of dollars to clean up.

The quality of the water we drink is only one water issue in the news. Another issue is the amount of available water. With an ever-increasing population comes an increasing demand for water. As we continue to use more surface and groundwater to meet the demands, such issues as land subsidence, degraded and dewatered streams and wetlands, and legal battles over water use and water-quality protection are more frequently in the news. Clean water is actually a limited resource, just like coal and oil.

THE SCIENCE

Where Does Our Drinking Water Come From?

Drinking water can be drawn from the ground or from surface bodies of water—lakes, rivers, or reservoirs (Figure 3.1). About 10 percent of Americans have private drinking wells that pump groundwater. People in cities get their drinking water from municipal water-treatment plants. Where does a municipal water plant obtain water? Municipal sources can include groundwater, rivers, lakes, and reservoirs. More than 273 million people receive water from 53,000 community water systems.[1] Bottled water can come from any of these sources.

What Is Groundwater?

Groundwater is the water that fills the spaces, or pores, between soil particles under the ground surface. Different soils can hold

Figure 3.1 Snowmelt runoff fills a reservoir in the Rocky Mountains near Dillon, Colorado. The largest water storage facility in the state, the Dillon Reservoir also serves as a great destination for recreational boating, camping, and fishing.

different amounts of water. Sands, gravels, and rock formations with large pore spaces that can hold large deposits of groundwater are called **aquifers**.

The top of the saturated layer, the area in which all the pore spaces are filled with water and contain no air, is called the **water table** (Figure 3.2). Wells are dug into the water table. A water table can be near the ground surface, as it is in a wetland, or it can be hundreds of feet below, as in a desert. It all depends on the lay of the land and the amount of water that drains into an area.

Where Does Groundwater Come From?

Groundwater comes from a variety of sources. When rain or snow falls, water can seep into the ground, be stored on the surface, or

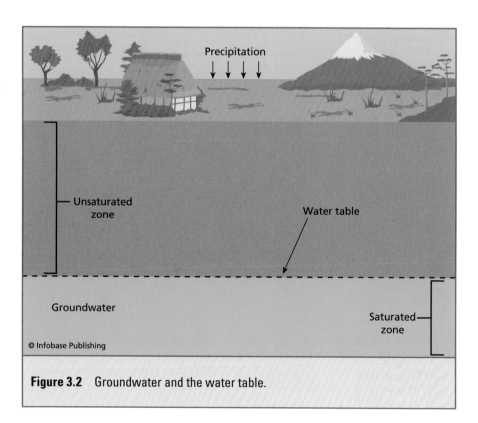

© Infobase Publishing

Figure 3.2 Groundwater and the water table.

run off to low-lying areas. Plant roots may capture a portion of the water that seeps into the soil, while the rest is stored between the soil particles. Surface water is stored in rivers, lakes, and wetlands. At certain times of the year, this surface water can percolate down to the groundwater. The sources and supplies of groundwater, however, are not without limits.

For example, the groundwater being pumped from the Ogallala Aquifer, an aquifer that runs through portions of eight states, is as old as the dinosaurs—quite literally, hundreds of millions of years old. People started drawing water for **irrigation** from the aquifer in the early 1900s. The water table has been falling ever since and, in some places, has been drained. Refilling of aquifers can take hundreds or even thousands of years. When that water is gone, it will not be replenished for many generations to come.

How Does Groundwater Move?

Groundwater does not flow like an underground river because it moves through the tiny spaces between the soil particles. The science of hydrology has brought us a better understanding of groundwater movement; yet, that movement can still be difficult to predict.

Water movement is affected by the physical features of the landscape and by the size of the soil particles. Gravity causes water to flow downhill. The rate at which it flows depends on how fast the soils can transmit, or move, the water. Sandy soils transmit water quickly, whereas clay soils trap water, so it moves very slowly, if at all.

Water movement depends on even more than soil type and landscape features. Water flows more quickly through saturated or wet soil than through partially wet or dry soil. The rate of movement also is affected by the thickness of the saturated zone of the water. In addition, groundwater flow can change direction. The force used in pumping water out of a well will, in turn, draw water toward the well (Figure 3.3).

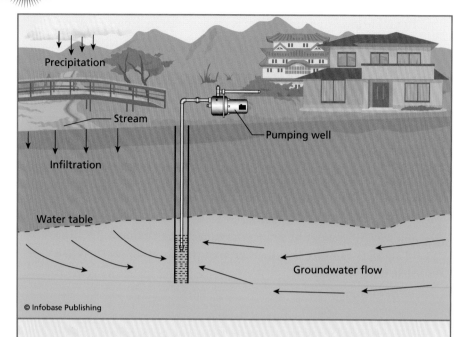

© Infobase Publishing

Figure 3.3 As wells pump water out of the ground, the level of the water table can drop. In addition, the pressure from pumping can draw water from nearby lakes and rivers into the well.

Are Surface Waters Connected to Wetlands and Groundwater?

The water in lakes, rivers, wetlands, and groundwater is all connected. The connection is not always the same—it can vary by season or climate conditions. In addition, the way in which all these sources of water interact is affected by the types of soils, the lay of the land, the geology, and human activities.

Sometimes groundwater contributes water to a surface-water body. For example, about half of the streams in the Chesapeake Bay watershed are fed by groundwater.[2] During times of drought or low water, groundwater may actually contribute water to wetlands, lakes, and rivers. Yet, when the surface waters or wetlands are filled with water after rains or snowmelt, the water flow may reverse, instead recharging, or refilling, the groundwater.

Whereas some changes in flow direction are natural, other changes are created by humans. For example, when large amounts of water are pumped from the ground, water may be drawn down, or sucked away, from nearby lakes, streams, or wetlands. As the United State Geological Survey noted in their 2001 Report on our Nation's Water Quality, groundwater contributions to America's streams and rivers can be substantial.[3] Humans can also change the water flow by diverting surface water for irrigation, domestic uses, or industrial uses, which may cause groundwater to lose a valuable source of recharge.

What Do Watersheds Have to Do with Drinking Water?

A watershed is the land area that contributes, or drains, water to a certain area. Water naturally is pulled by gravity to a low point. So water or snow falling on a mountain eventually makes its way down the mountain to a stream or lake. The land over which this water drains is called the watershed.

What do watersheds have to do with drinking water? For one thing, the water from rain and snow and from rivers and streams recharges, or refills, the drinking-water sources—both surface waters and groundwater. For another, if the watershed is on the side of a mountain range where not much rain falls, drinking-water sources may be in short supply.

In addition, water flowing over the land carries contamination in the watershed to lakes, streams, wetlands, and groundwater. Contaminants include pollutants dissolved in the water, such as pesticides or heavy metals, and sediment.

Scientists have given policymakers the information needed to make better planning decisions that protect our environment and the associated economic resources. Policymakers are now designing water-quality protection programs that consider what is happening in the whole watershed. Even forest managers recognize the connection between water and land use. Mike Dombeck, former chief of the United States Forest Service, said, "The focus should be on how to let our forests do their job of producing high-quality water. Given our water supply problems, this should be the highest priority of forest management."[4]

Do Wetlands Protect America's Drinking-Water Sources?

Wetlands protect America's drinking-water sources in two critical ways: improving water quality and increasing water quantity.

A major function of wetlands is improving water quality. Wetlands are located in low-lying areas, and, thus, water tends to remain there for a period of time, which is called *residence time*. This allows physical settling of sediments, while also allowing the time necessary for many biological and chemical reactions to occur that can remove more pollutants. For example, anaerobic bacteria that live in wetlands convert nitrate, a contaminant, into nitrogen gas, which makes up 78 percent of our atmosphere. Some cities are building wetlands to help take nitrogen out of waste water before the water is discharged into rivers or lakes. In addition, wetland plants and organic soils can sequester, or trap, heavy metals and other pollutants.

The other important way that wetlands protect our drinking water is by increasing water quantity; in other words, by recharging, or refilling, lakes, streams, and groundwater.

What Are the Threats to Drinking Water?

Many sources of contamination to surface water, groundwater, and wetlands exist. Among these threats are leaking landfills and petroleum storage tanks, discharges into the air and water from industries, large agricultural operations, sewage-treatment plant discharges, mining, and some business operations (Figure 3.4). In addition, the EPA keeps a list of common pollutants found at Superfund sites (areas designated for hazardous-waste cleanup), including chemicals, metals, and other substances.

Pollutants are not always directly discharged to the water or land. One threat to water quality comes from the air, via emissions from coal-burning industries and power plants. Sulfur

Figure 3.4   This 1928 photograph shows sewage flowing into the Mississippi River in Minneapolis, Minnesota. This image was used by the Minnesota Board of Health to teach its State Public Health officials how to properly dispose of waste in order to prevent disease.

and nitrous oxides fall to the water as acid rain. Mercury, another product of burning coal, also falls to the water, where bacteria change it to methylmercury, a powerful neurotoxin that affects brain function.

Nonpoint Source Pollution

Nonpoint source pollution is any pollution that does not come from a specific point, or source, such as a factory, leaking storage tank, or landfill. The phrase *nonpoint source pollution* covers all the contaminants that are picked up by rain or melting snow and transported to surface and groundwater. For example, salt, sediment, oils, greases, agricultural runoff from fields (animals wastes, fertilizers, and pesticides), and runoff from domestic practices are nonpoint source pollution (Figure 3.5). The EPA has identified

Figure 3.5 Technician Jeff Nichols collects a sample of water from a watershed to check for contaminated water. The technician collects samples every week to determine if farming practices are affecting the water quality.

nonpoint source pollution as the number-one source of pollution to America's water.[5] It also states that these pollutants can have harmful effects on drinking-water supplies. A recent report by the United States Geological Survey states that pesticides occur in our streams in quantities that "may have effects on aquatic life or fish-eating wildlife."[6]

Global Warming

Climate changes alter weather patterns and the way water falls to the ground. Shifting rainfall patterns mean that some areas may experience water shortages.

With continued warming and the melting of glaciers come intensifying rains and droughts, warns Mario Molina, a 1995 Nobel Prize–winning chemist, whose research warned us of the dangers of chlorofluorocarbons (CFCs) destroying the ozone layer.[7] His warnings were presented during an international meeting in Mexico City in March, 2006, of UNESCO (United Nations Educational Scientific and Cultural Organization) to mark Water World Day 2006.

Does Groundwater Pollution Differ from Surface-Water Pollution?

Groundwater pollution differs from surface-water pollution in several important ways. When a river or lake becomes polluted, the effects are easy to see: the water's appearance changes (color, smell, and algae growth), and the death of some fish and plants is often observed. The difficulty with identifying groundwater contamination, of course, is that it occurs under the ground, away from our direct observation.

Often, the contamination is not identified until some major problem has been traced back to a drinking-water supply. By that time, remediation of the pollution may not be possible, because the cleansing of groundwater is very expensive and difficult.

Another way in which groundwater pollution differs from that of surface water is in the way the water moves. In rivers and streams, water flows downstream in a riverbed, and in lakes, water mixes within a lake basin. Movement of groundwater depends on a different set of variables that are not always easy to predict.

All these reasons contribute to the difficulty and expense of cleaning up contaminated groundwater. As an example, American Pacific Corporation is planning a 45-year project to clean up an ammonium perchlorate contamination site in Nevada. In addition to the long time period needed to clean the groundwater, the project will cost $8 million the first year, and $800,000 each year after that to pump the contaminated groundwater out, clean it, and reinject it into the ground.[8]

What Are the Health Effects of Drinking Contaminated Water?

The EPA states that the negative health effects of drinking contaminated water include immediate adverse health effects in addition to "chronic effects that may occur if contaminants are ingested at unsafe levels over many years."[9] The EPA identifies a wide range of health issues, depending on the contaminants. Included are intestinal problems; increased risk of cancers; hair loss; damage to the liver, kidneys, and intestines; neurologic and reproductive problems; cataracts; and immune deficiencies.[10]

What Is Considered "Safe" Drinking Water?

For the more than 15 million Americans who get their water from private wells, what constitutes safe drinking water is their call. The government does not test or regulate wells that serve fewer than 25 people.

For drinking-water sources that serve more than 25 people, the EPA sets drinking-water standards, in compliance with the Safe Drinking Water Act (SDWA). These legally enforceable standards are called the National Primary Drinking Water Regulations (NPDWRs, or primary standards). Standards have been set for 90 chemical, microbiological, radiological, and physical contaminants in drinking water.[11] Approximately 90 percent of the municipal water systems meet these quality standards.[12]

The EPA works with other groups to research which currently unregulated contaminants constitute threats to public health and should be regulated. Since the SDWA was passed, more contaminants are continually added to the list of those regulated.

Note, however, that the EPA qualifies that drinking water that meets SDWA standards is "generally" safe. Certain populations, for example infants, older people, and those who are ill, are more susceptible to chemicals and other contaminants. The EPA cautions these people to consult with their health-care providers regarding the safety of their drinking water.[13]

What Is Land Subsidence?

Land subsidence is a condition in which land subsides, or sinks, because too much water has been pumped out of the ground. Soil, the stuff beneath our feet, has three components: the solids of the soil, the air in the spaces between the solids, and water filling those spaces. When the spaces between the soil particles are filled with water, a stable base exists on which people can build roads and homes. However, pumping too much water out of the ground leaves only the air spaces and the soil particles. The land actually sinks as the soil shifts and collapses—in some places sinking many feet. Land subsidence is becoming an increasing problem in several states, including Arizona, Florida, and California.

What Is Desalination?

Desalination is a process in which salt water is filtered to yield water suitable for drinking and irrigation (Figure 3.6). Removal of the excess salts and minerals from seawater can be accomplished by different methods. Most of the desalination plants are in the Middle East, but more are being built in the United States.

Although a lot of water is contained in the oceans, the desalination process is expensive. The cost is approximately three to

Figure 3.6 An employee pours a sample of water at a desalination plant in El Segundo, California. The desalination system forces seawater through high pressure filters, which results in clean, drinkable water.

five times more to process salt water than to treat freshwater. In addition, the process uses a lot of energy. It also produces a hypersaline brine that is classified by the EPA as industrial waste. Some concerns exist about the effects on ocean ecosystems of pumping large amounts of water and then returning desalinated water to the ocean. Another concern is the potential effects of pumping large amounts of water out of an ocean ecosystem.

HISTORY OF THE ISSUE

Water Quality

Two methods are available by which to ensure that the water Americans drink from public wells is safe. One method is to monitor and regulate the quality of the water coming from municipal wells. The second method is to prevent the pollutants from entering the water supply in the first place. The Safe Drinking Water Act regulates the quality of the water from the wells, and the Clean Water Act regulates activities that could pollute the drinking-water sources.

The Safe Drinking Water Act

The first formal attempts at regulating water supplies for health reasons were in 1914, when the U.S. Public Health Service set standards to prevent the spread of communicable diseases. These standards were not mandatory and only addressed diseases spread by bacteria. In 1925, several heavy metals were added to the list. By 1962, a total of 28 contaminants were included in the recommended standards. Not until 1974 did Congress pass the Safe Drinking Water Act, which set mandatory compliance standards for drinking wells that served more than 25 people. This law covers water from both aboveground or underground sources, either being used, or having the potential for being used, as drinking water.[14]

By the early 1980s, 83 contaminants were listed. In 1996, the Congress reauthorized the SDWA, which established a process for adding new contaminants to the list.

The Clean Water Act

Until the 1970s, the policies and regulations in our country supported the development of industry, agriculture, and population centers. America was a land of plenty, and water seemed an unlimited resource to be used for economic gain. Our nation's policies were designed to fill wetlands, build dams, and allow unregulated industrial discharges of pollutants. This attitude was typified in President Herbert Hoover's comment, "Every drop of water that runs to the sea without yielding its full commercial returns to the nation is an economic waste."[15]

The attitude of unbridled development began to change after the Cuyahoga River, near Lake Erie, caught fire in 1969 (Figure 3.7). Americans demanded regulations to protect their waterways—75 percent of which, at that time, were unfit for swimming, fishing, or drinking. In 1972, Congress passed the Clean Water Act (CWA): "The objective of this Act is to restore and maintain the chemical, physical, and biological integrity of the Nation's waters."[16] The CWA regulated such point sources as discharges from sewage-treatment plants and industries. It also contained a section to protect what remained of our nation's wetlands, important ecosystems for improving water quality. In the 1980s, the EPA started to address nonpoint sources of water pollution—the runoff after rain or snow events from streets, farms, and construction sites.

In the 1990s, the EPA began to shift from source or program regulation to a watershed approach, taking into account everything that was happening in the area that contributed to water bodies. The policy shift is still reflected today in the water-protection strategies of the EPA.

Water Quantity

Neither the Safe Drinking Water Act nor the Clean Water Act addresses drinking-water quantity, meaning the amount of water available. As the United States became more industrialized, the water needs grew and often competed with each other. The doctrine of "reasonable use" came to be the rule of thumb for using

Figure 3.7 In 1969, the Cuyahoga River caught fire due to illegal dumping of waste in the water. In this image, firefighters work to tame the fire, which ultimately destroyed three tugboats, three buildings, and the ship repair yards.

water in the eastern part of the country. It meant that if the water use benefited the community economically, the use was reasonable and, therefore, was not limited. It also meant that if a new activity had more community value, the new user could take the water of a prior user. For example, a new industry could take the water from an older, smaller one.

As the western states developed, however, they began, and continue today, to operate under a much different doctrine of water use. During the 1800s, and into the 1900s, mining and agriculture in the West demanded huge quantities of water. The government, at all levels, wanted to promote both activities for economic reasons. The doctrine of "prior appropriation" became the rule in the West, which meant "first-in-time, first-in-right," or the first person to claim the water has unlimited rights to use it.[17] The policy continues to today in the western United States and has a direct effect on the quantity of groundwater available for drinking water.

CURRENT ISSUES AND FUTURE CONSIDERATIONS

Water Quality

Historically, the Clean Water Act addresses point sources of pollution—for example, industrial discharges, sewage-treatment plants, and large animal-feeding operations. Section 404 was added to protect wetlands, in recognition of the key role wetlands play in water quality and keeping ecosystems healthy. A current issue is the Supreme Court's June 2006 decision (*Rapanos v. United States*) to exempt isolated wetlands from protection under the Clean Water Act.

Current and future considerations are the success of the various programs being introduced to control nonpoint source pollution and to address water quality on a watershed basis. The watershed approach recognizes the importance of protecting watersheds while they are still healthy and of restoring damaged systems.[18]

With increased funding and improved detection methods, the EPA has established a threefold increase in the number of contaminants regulated under the Safe Drinking Water Act since 1974. The EPA estimates that about 90 percent of public water supplies currently meet federal standards. Improving the quality of the remaining systems and keeping the others up to standard is a current and future concern. Monitoring of, and providing financial assistance to, public water companies continues to be a goal of the EPA. Since the last revision of the SDWA in 1996, the EPA has provided $8 billion to local water systems to help them meet these goals.[19] In addition, the EPA continues to add contaminants to their list as scientific research and economic considerations allow.

Water Quantity

Whether the Eastern policy of "reasonable use" or the Western policy of "prior appropriation" (first come, first served) governs water withdrawals, water quantity is becoming an increasingly contentious issue. The water wars, as they have been called, are being fought in courtrooms around the nation. Such questions as whether you can pump water from the ground if it makes your neighbor's pond go dry, or whether you can pump water from your pond if it dries up your neighbor's well, are legal questions that increasingly rely on science for an answer. Should water be pumped from one watershed into another to feed a growing population's water needs? Should water bottlers be able to pump as much water as they want at the expense of the wetlands or surface water in a wildlife refuge?

As scientists continue to document the strong connections among all water sources—ground and surface—the legal decisions are being closely watched. Science also tells us that aquifer water supplies are limited, and because of this, the question of who gets to use how much water takes on increased importance.

Economics

The bottom line, which comes down to economics, is that most of our drinking water costs money. As cities attempt to meet increased water demands, construction of pipelines and the pumping of water from other watersheds will only increase the cost of water. In addition, contaminated water adds millions of dollars to associated health-care costs, ecosystem damage, and clean-up expenses. As an example, in August of 2005, the EPA reached a $28-million settlement with United Technologies, Inc. to clean up their contamination of a shallow groundwater system at a site in California.[20]

Protection of drinking water supplies also costs money, but cities are finding that protection is always less expensive than cleaning dirty water. For example, more than six cities have avoided the costs of billion-dollar treatment plants by investing in watershed protection. New York City spent $1.5 billion over

10 years by buying forest land to protect the watershed of its drinking-water source. The investment saved them the initial $6-billion cost of constructing a treatment plant and $300,000 in annual operation costs.[21]

In 2005, the Massachusetts Water Resources Authority (MWRA) released numbers that showed a remarkable trend. Despite increased economic growth and little population change in the Boston area, the demand for water has decreased to a 50-year low. The MWRA was able to avoid diverting water from the Connecticut River by pursuing a strong conservation program in 1987. These actions saved the MWRA's more than 2,000,000 customers more than $500 million in capital spending alone.

WHAT THE INDIVIDUAL CAN DO

We can all work together to reduce and prevent nonpoint source pollution. Some activities are federal responsibilities, such as ensuring that federal lands are properly managed to reduce soil erosion. Some activities are state responsibilities, such as developing legislation to govern mining and logging and to protect groundwater. Other strategies are best handled locally, by such means as zoning or erosion control ordinances. Each individual can play an important role by practicing conservation and by changing everyday habits.

REFERENCES

1. U.S. Environmental Protection Agency. "Safe Drinking Water Act." Available online. URL: http://www.epa.gov/safewater/sdwa/30th/index.html. 2005.

2. United States Geological Survey. "Water quality in the nations streams and aquifers." Available online. URL: http://water.usgs.gov/nawqa/. 2004.

3. United States Geological Survey. "Water quality in the nations streams and aquifers." Available online. URL: http://water.usgs.gov/nawqa/. 2004.

4. Postel, Sandra. *Liquid Assests: The Critical Need to Safeguard Freshwater Ecosystems. Worldwatch Paper 170.* Washington D.C.: Worldwatch Institute, 2005.

5. U.S. EPA. "Factsheet: Nonpoint source pollution," EPA841-F-96-004A. Available online. URL: http://www.epa.gov/owow/nps/facts/point1.htm.

6. United States Geological Survey. "Pesticides in the nation's streams and groundwater." Available online. URL: http://pubs.usgs.gov/fs/2006/3028/pdf/fs2006-3028.pdf. 2006.

7. Environmental New Service. "Global warming will make water crisis intolerable." Available online. URL: http://www.ens-newswire.com/ens/mar2006/2006-03-22-01.asp. 2006.

8. "Henderson rocket fuel manufacturer planning perchlorate clean-up," Reno Gazette Journal. Available online. URL: http://www.rgj.com/news/stories/html/2005/08/13/106349.php?sps=rgj.com&sch=LocalNews&sp1=rgj&sp2=News&sp3=Local+News&sp5=RGJ.com&sp6=news&sp7=local_news. 2005.

9. U.S. Environmental Protection Agency. "Safe Drinking Water Act 30th anniversary drinking water standards & health effects." Available online. URL: http://www.epa.gov/safewater/sdwa/30th/factsheets/standard.html#4. 2004.

10. U.S. Environmental Protection Agency. "Groundwater and drinking water list of drinking water contaminants & MCLs. National primary drinking water regulations." Available online. URL: http://www.epa.gov/safewater/mcl.html. 2006.

11. U.S. Environmental Protection Agency. "Safe Drinking Water Act 30th anniversary drinking water standards & health effects." Available online. URL: http://www.epa.gov/safewater/sdwa/30th/factsheets/standard.html#4. 2004.

12. U.S. Environmental Protection Agency. "Safe Drinking Water Act." Available online. URL: http://www.epa.gov/safewater/sdwa/30th/index.html. 2005.

13. U.S. Environmental Protection Agency. "Safe Drinking Water Act 30th anniversary drinking water standards & health effects." Available online. URL: http://www.epa.gov/safewater/sdwa/30th/factsheets/standard.html#4. 2004.

14. U.S. Environmental Protection Agency. "Safe Drinking Water Act." Available online. URL: http://www.epa.gov/region5/defs/html/sdwa.htm. 2006.

15. Glennon, Robert. *Water Follies: Groundwater Pumping and the Fate of America's Fresh Waters*. Washington, D.C.: Island Press, 2002.

16. U.S. Environmental Protection Agency. "Federal Water Pollution Control Act (as amended 2002) (33 U.S.C. 1251 et seq.)." Available online. URL: http://www.epa.gov/region5/water/pdf/ecwa.pdf. 2002.

17. Glennon, *Water Follies*, p. 30.

18. U.S. Environmental Protection Agency. "Introduction to the Clean Water Act." Available online. URL: http://www.epa.gov/watertrain/cwa/. 2003.

19. U.S. Environmental Protection Agency. "Safe Drinking Water Act." Available online. URL: http://www.epa.gov/safewater/sdwa/30th/index.html. 2005.

20. "U.S. EPA reaches major settlement for cleanup of San Gabriel Valley Superfund site." Press Release. U.S. EPA Region 9, August 22, 2005.

21. Postel, *Liquid Assests*, p. 6.

FURTHER READING

Books

Gleick, Peter H. *The World's Water: 2004–2005. The Biennial Report on Freshwater Resources.* Washington, D.C.: Island Press, 2004.

Glennon, Robert: *Groundwater Pumping and the Fate of America's Fresh Waters.* Washington, D.C.: Island Press, 2002.

Postel, Sandra. *Liquid Assets: The Critical Need to Safeguard Freshwater Ecosystems. Worldwatch Paper 170.* Washington, D.C.: Worldwatch Institute, 2005.

Postel, Sandra and Brian Richter. *Rivers for Life: Managing Water for People and Nature.* Washington D.C.: Island Press, 2003.

Web Sites

The Nature Conservancy
http://www.nature.org/initiatives/freshwater/strategies/cities.html

United States Environmental Protection Agency
www.epa.gov/water/

United States Geological Survey
http://water.usgs.gov/nawqa/

GLOSSARY

Anaerobic Chemical processes that occur in the absence of oxygen.

Aquifer An underground area of soil, usually consisting of sand and gravel, that holds and transmits large amounts of water.

Biodiversity A term coined in the 1980s to mean biological diversity; the diversity of living things; the term refers to diversity on three levels: ecosystem diversity, species diversity, and genetic diversity.

Bog A wetland with no significant water flowing in or out; bogs accumulate acid-loving mosses like sphagnum and have organic soils.

Ecosystem The interaction among the living (plants, animals, and microorganisms) and the nonliving (soil, air, weather, water, and sunlight) components in an area.

Erosion The process by which forces of water, wind, or ice wear away or transport rocks and soil.

Estuary The area where fresh water mixes with salt water, creating a brackish environment.

Fen A peat-accumulating wetland with some water inflow from surrounding areas and that usually has marsh-like vegetation.

Greenhouse gas A gas that absorbs infrared energy, which creates a warm layer of air around the Earth. Carbon dioxide, methane, nitrous oxide, water vapor, and fluorinated gases are examples.

Hydrology The study of the movement, quality, and distribution of water.

Irrigation The process of diverting water from natural sources (groundwater, rivers, or lakes) to provide water for agricultural or other human uses.

Mitigation A method of decreasing the environmental impacts of development to ecosystems (usually wetlands) by attempting to replace or restore similar ecosystems.

≡GLOSSARY≡

Muskeg Vast area of peatland or bog; most common in Canada and Alaska.

Nonpoint source pollution Pollution from indirect sources, caused when rain or snowmelt flows over the land and collects contaminants; includes run-off from agricultural areas or roads, septic systems, construction sites, and acid rain.

Ozone A molecule consisting of three atoms of oxygen created in a heat-driven chemical reaction in the atmosphere. In the stratosphere, it protects the Earth from harmful radiation. Close to the ground surface, it is an air pollutant.

Photosynthesis The chemical process by which light energy from the sun powers a reaction that chemically changes water and carbon dioxide into glucose.

Pocosin Peat-accumulating freshwater wetland that supports evergreen shrubs and trees; primarily found in the southeastern United States.

Salinity The measure of dissolved salts in a water body.

Prairie pothole A shallow, marsh-like wetland, mostly located in the Dakotas and middle Canadian provinces.

Salt marsh A coastal area inundated with tidal salt water twice daily, supporting grasses and other plants that thrive in the brackish environment.

Sediment Particle matter resulting from the weathering of rocks and soils by physical and chemical processes.

Swamp A wetland dominated by woody vegetation; also called a forested wetland.

Vernal pool A wetland found in a shallow depression filled with water during certain seasons, usually spring, and dry during the summer. Vernal pools provide a valuable breeding environment or feeding area for many species of plants and animals.

Water table The top layer of the saturated zone in which all the pore spaces are filled with water; the upper surface of the groundwater.

Watershed An area of land that drains into a body of water.

Wetland Land that has standing water for certain periods during the year, hydric soils, and supports wetland vegetation.

PICTURE CREDITS

INDEX

=INDEX

= ABOUT THE AUTHOR =

YAEL CALHOUN is a graduate of Brown University. She has an M.A. in education and a M.S. in natural resources science. Years of work as an environmental planner have provided her with much experience in environmental issues at the local, state, and federal level. Currently, she writes books and teaches environmental biology at Westminster College in Salt Lake City. She lives with her family at the foot of the Rocky Mountains in Utah.